Editions DIASPORAS NOIRES

www.diasporas-noires.com

©MIR - International Movement for Reparations 2020

ISBN digital version: 9782490931187

ISBN printed version : 9782490931194

Digital Publication Date : September 2020

Cover image: Designed in 2018 by Sathérou Seba and Mame Hulo for the 1st Konvwa in Africa, this image of a man with his broken chains, accompanied by his wife returning by sea, here in Goree, symbolizes a victory over all the so-called "**gates of NO RETURN**" that abound on the Continent. The descendants of the African deportees **are of RETURN** and this is a major reparation !

REPARATIONS

An urgent requirement for Humanity

COLLECTIVE INTERNATIONAL BOOK
Highlighting the 20th
KONVWA BA REPARASYON
May 2020 in Martinique

Work coordinated by MIR

(Mouvement International pour les Réparations/International Movement for Reparations)

Garcin Malsa & Mame Hulo

With the invaluable help of Myriam Malsa

Translated from French by Joséphine Ndiaye

REPARATIONS

An urgent requirement for humanity

Philippe Bessière - Nita Brochant

Gladys Démocrite - Patricia Donatien

Queen Mother Dòwòti Désir - Claudette Duhamel

René Louis Parfait Etilé - Mame Hulo - Jacqueline Jacqueray

Apa Mumia Makeba - Garcin Malsa - Alain Manville

Rosa Amelia Plumelle-Uribe - Luc Reinette

Pr Coovi Rekhmiré - Louis Sala-Molins

Juliette Smeralda - Rodolphe Solbiac

Joby Valente

DIASPORAS NOIRES
Collection Racines

LIST OF AUTHORS

(classified by order of appearance of their written contributions) :

Garcin Malsa - Martinique

Chairman of MIR International

International Movement for Reparations

Claudette Duhamel - Martinique

Lawyer and Vice-President of MIR

Alain Manville - Martinique

Lawyer and member of MIR

Pr Coovi Rekhimre - Benin

Egyptologist, Philosopher and Historian.

Specialist of the European Negro Trafficking

Rodolphe Solbiac - Martinique

Lecturer, Habilitated to supervise research

English Caribbean Studies - University of the West Indies

Rosa Amelia Plumelle-Uribe - Colombia

Colombian, Author of several books on the slave trade, slavery and colonial domination.

René Louis Parfait Etile - Martinique

Egyptologist from Martinique

Louis Sala-Molins – France

Professor of Political Philosophy, specialist in the practices of the Roman Inquisition and the codification of black slavery

Mame Hulo (Guillabert) - Senegal

Writer, Director of Diasporas Noires Editions,

Member of the Pan-African Federalist Movement Ambassador for Africa of the MIR

Philippe Bessière – Reunion Island

For the Komité Rényoné Panafrikin & MIR Réunion

Nita Brochant, Jaklin Jacqueray, Luc Reinette - Guadeloupe

The Drafting Committee of the ICNP International Committee of Black People

Gladys Démocrite - Guadeloupe

Lawyer - Member of the ICNP International Committee of Black People

Her Majesty Queen Mother Dòwòti Désir Hounon Houna II Guely - Haiti/Benin

The Afro-Atlantic Theologies & Treaties Institute

Juliette Sméralda - Martinique

Sociologist, writer, researcher

Apa Mumia Makeba (Benoît Bechet) – French Guiana

Chairman of MIR French Guiana

Patricia Donatien - Martinique

University Professor

University of the West Indies

Joby Valente - France

President of the Movement for a New Humanity

Vice President of the Collectif des Filles et Fils d'Africains Déportés (Collective of Daughters and sons of African Deportees)

TABLES OF CONTENTS

REPARATIONS —An an urgent requirement for humanity

Introduction

By Garcin Malsa

Chairman of MIR International
International Movement for Reparations

For more than a decade now, the oppressed have been experiencing a growing need for justice, for humanity, for truth. In the same time, all types of political dynasties dressed up as democracies, which in fact are representing neo conservative ideologies, were tending to be systematically rejected -for being oblivious of the fact that people's memories, despite the fact that they have been deprived of everything else, remain alive. Advocacy of these ideologies has in fact been attributed to the occidental world.

More and more people are now turning their back to these leaders who were involving them in this neo conservative path. Isn't it obvious that this fragmented world, the fruit of clash of religions, of various culture and, civilizations is actually getting tired of all this? We are presently looking at the end of a world that is getting old and dehumanized, a dying world.

It is as if demonstrations that have occurred, might they have been violent or not, were just expressing far too much suffering from a ransacked and now erupting planet.

An erupting planet, civil wars – a dying world

As we have been crossing a different path, as far as history, culture, sociology are concerned, the African people, whereas in the continent or in the diaspora, considering all cultural mutations we have been through, should find a way to contribute to the birth of a new world to come, with more justice, humanity, solidarity, devoted to the living and ecology.

That is what the International Movement for Reparations (MIR) is about.

Prior to talking about MIR, I first want to pay a tribute to a great thinker whose writings have been inspiring to a great many pan Africanists, **Antenor FIRMIN**.

In his book, "About Racial Equality", written as an answer to GOBINEAU's book "About Racial Inequalities" he gives scientifically proved facts to wipe away GOBINEAU's racist and subjective thesis on human race.

He also proved to be a real visionary in the way he addressed to Haiti in the same book: *"...May this book be an inspiration to love for progress, justice and freedom for all the children of the black human race! For by addressing it to Haiti, I am also refering to today's destitutes and tomorrow giants"*.

I am quite satisfied to realize that protesters movements against colonial establishment in Africa, such as the refusal of CFA franc, claims of national sovereignty for African states, land claim settlement in South Africa, etc., are an answer more than 135 years after the book was released to the call of Antenor FIRMIN.

I have also been able to observe that all these demonstrations of civil disobedience in Guadeloupe and Guyana by activists, were launched according to the wish of Antenor FIRMIN.

And then again, I am able to observe that movements of boycott against shopping centers, started by Martinican people to fight landowners' attempt to poison them with pesticides like chlordecone were launched according to the wish of Antenor FIRMIN call.

It is as if all these activists, most of all just young people, organized as they may, raging against injustices undergone by their people for more than four centuries now, were becoming the embodiment of so much suffering that has been taking place since black slavery had occurred. And now the amount of the suffering is expressed through righteous civil wars.

Seeing them in this process, one cannot but think to the oath taken in **Bois Kaiman**, a spiritual preparation to the battle leading to the ultimate victory.

While protesters are now making calls for convergence in the struggle to demand justice and reparations, MIR is making a call to African people in the continent and in the diaspora for a voluntarist approach in order to meet and reconnect.

Where there is Reconnection, there necessarily is convergence, and Self-Reparation.

We cannot but add Reparation to all this.

MIR's requirement for Reparation is an integral part of DECOLONIZATION.

Thus allowing SOVEREIGNTY to be part of it.

This is MIR's self-assigned mission, since it has been created. Besides, well before that, its founding members had engaged western countries in 1992 by including the 3 R in their actions for Decolonization: **Recognition of crime, Reparation and Reconciliation.**

No prophecy, no messianic posturing, no coincidence.

Time has come for our ancestors to bring together their fruitful source of energy and fill us with it to reach every form of self-reparation while opening the way for thorough and integral Reparation. This will benefit the whole planet by bringing it well-being.

This is why I am addressing this call to all fair-minded people in the world to magnify actions already taken by MIR and bring them to international level.
In 2005, MIR Martinique brought an action against the French state for reparation following the constitution of a two-crimes commission and the designation of a college of experts to ultimately have a full knowledge of this hidden part of history.

A provision of 20 billion euros was requested and a college of experts convened to evaluate and expertise damages

This judicial initiative had not been taken seriously at the time and was even treated with sarcasm both by the press and the French state.

It was unanimously considered a bad joke.

Ten years later, the joke had become one of the most serious questions asked to the French state and, legal action initiated on all fronts, the provisional amount of 20 billion euros that some had found amusing then, now left them with no other option than to grin and bear it.

Over ten years later, the French state has no other option than taking the issue seriously and admit the relevance of these legal procedures taken to the French court and, acknowledge before the two-crimes commission, its responsibility despite scandalous and revisionist denial of the French state.

However, there was a lack of courage on the French government side, to reconcile the rigor of the criminal law which made it backed away about the compensation issue.
The French government denied any compensation on the grounds that it was subject to a prescription limit under French law and that TAUBIRA law also excluded financial compensation. There was an appeal against the judgment. The French jurisdiction confirmed the lower court decision.

The European Court of Human Rights has just declared the MIR request admissible, in February 2020. This is a first victory for the MIR and a slap in the face for the French government.

Obviously the two arguments put forward by both the Court and the French state do not withstand close examination, that crimes against humanity cannot be subject to statutory limitations, neither are integral rights for compensation which are inherently linked, that TAUBIRA law cannot by nature exclude any right to financial compensation of the two crimes without violating the constitutional principles ensuring every victim to receive compensation and not be discriminated.

In applying the law, there is no way to lose the fight, for it is just a question of time to compel judges to rule accordingly and not only order an expert to report but also sentence the French state to bear its costs.

Legally speaking, it is inevitable for the French State to be sentenced, the judges' ideological resistance together with their fear of being unfaithful to the French Nation as the good civil servants they are need to be forced open.

MIR Martinique, has been committing itself to fighting this war for over 15 years now and needs to step up to broaden the scope of its activities with an efficient tool.

At this stage the reparation issue is a timely theme that absolutely needs to be solved now, for those who are not in favour of reparations having understood that such an issue cannot be avoided, have already chosen to reshuffle the cards.

Many organizations have opened their own workcamps, in which however reparation does rhyme with reconciliation and excludes financial compensation, in line with that of the French State, which only intends to provide a memory compensation that it does not otherwise assume.

The issue of the two crimes would therefore be considered a simple moral issue when the duty of memory is at stake.

These revisionists and servile ideologues at the service of the French state will increasingly occupy the media field and the fight initiated by MIR Martinique must be raised to another level.

This is why it was decided to create MIR International whose founding members will be international personalities who want the French State to finally pay its debt to the rightful heirs of the victims of both crimes.

The creation of this organization is a response to the current state of affairs.

The issue has been brought to the very UN by several sovereign Caribbean States.

Some heads of state are denouncing the system of domination and violent exploitation to which the West is subjecting the African continent. The white world and all its institutions are in fact working to maintain their shameless exploitation of the world.

The question of reparation is not only that of the two crimes of slavery and slave trade, the slave trade having been the most violent form of this exploitation that the West has been pursuing for 5 centuries in the other part of the world.

It concerns the whole world which has suffered the domination of Western civilization built according to a racialized, reductive model, on the top of which stands the white man. The white man, setting himself up as a master profiteer from the exploitation of the planet and its ecosystems, has led it to disturbances and its consequences on the existence of the living. An intolerable world.

Time has come for the peoples who have been exploited, expropriated from their natural resources, to demand compensation from those who have plundered them. The crime was not only the physical violence, multiple genocides and the death of millions of people, which are part of the civilizational balance sheet of Western societies.

The violence was also fundamentally both economic and political.

The crime has also been the systematic looting and misappropriation of another's wealth for its sole benefit.

The peoples' debt has been kept gigantic for 4 centuries. In the midst of this drama, Africa has been undergoing the greatest global plundering that humanity has ever known. The debtor is none other than the West itself...

Sooner or later the West will have to pay its debt just as the French State will have to pay for the commission of the two crimes recognized by the TAUBIRA Law.

The face of the world is going to change as well as the balance of power which has meant that until now, nation states have been servile and subject to the demands and power of the West.

The West will have to be made accountable, and this accountability will involve the question of reparation.

The legal question brought before the French courts thus opens the way to putting into perspective the political relations that continue to endure and keep most of the world in a state of servility.

All of this needs to go public at International level, since the procedure itself has an international scope: international scope, not only because it is a world first and a unique case in the systems of rights existing on the planet up till now, but because it is a procedure that concerns and interests the totality of the Diaspora living throughout the world composed of African descent and African populations in the whole, which more than five centuries ago and, for three centuries, have been used as a workpower for the capitalist development of the European and North American powers.

This ebony wood was the first resource upon which the wealth of the western world was built.

It is now a matter of historic urgency that an organization whose scope covers the whole planet, be created and finds financial means and the good will to lead this fight for reparation, the first step of which are these procedures which claim reparation from the French State, but whose object is the questioning of the domination of the West over the world and the refusal henceforth of the balance of power to which the great majority of Humanity has been forced for the sole benefit of a few.

MIR Martinique must grow and create a political corpus that is equal to the question of reparation, which is today international, if not global in nature.

The creation of an international MIR that will have the capacity to intervene on this scale of reality will be the best guarantee that the fight that begun in 2005 against the French state can achieve its goals, but also that the question of reparation can become the driving issue of global politics in the 21st century.

While the civil rights issue in the 1960s in the United States advanced the cause of blacks, it has not in any way solved the black question.

Being black is still a state in the United States in which everyone is liable to experience violent death.

The question of reparation is an issue that cannot be overcome, cannot be integrated, cannot be unmanageable for the current system of world domination because it touches on its foundation: money and the power it gives.

The realignments of power and wealth that have taken place between the oil-producing countries and the West have not changed the logic of the system, as these countries have integrated themselves into its mechanism and made themselves one of its main investors.

The West, facing the question of reparation and the debt to be settled, will no longer be able to exercise its domination. Without money, there is no power.

The creation of **MIR International** will therefore raise the fight for reparation to its true historical dimension, that of a promoter of a revolution in the balance of power instituted by the Western powers.

The assassination of KHADAFI did not happen randomly, but only occurred because his will to create an African bank was considered a threat to the racket system of the CFA franc which would have enabled the African continent to escape from the big international banks that have been holding Africa through a fictitious debt.

How could Africa, which has been plundered for several centuries, have a debt to the one that has been stealing its wealth?

This is a legal fact acknowledged only by a few, and a platitude of common sense that escapes the latter, to one who is convinced that Africa may owe something to the West.

The West was well aware of the danger represented by this questioning of the fixed situation in the submission of African States to supranational interests.

The main task of MIR international in the field of the problem of the upheaval of the dominant world order today will be to enable the action for reparation against one of the main criminal exploiters of the construction of Western power to succeed and to force the French State to finally pay the debt it has been accumulating for more than 5 centuries.

The question of financial reparation, which the French State stubbornly refuses to consider will find, through **MIR International** action, the assent if not the positive support of all those who are aware of what has made the history of our world for several centuries: the excessive exploitation of the dominated.

In addition to making the fight against the French State visible and public at the international level, **MIR International** will also work to ensure that the world Diaspora of the beneficiaries of the victims of the two crimes can personally come and claim reparation from the French State, the only State in the world that is confronted with legal means that allow it to be condemned.

MIR International's mission will be to work with the States that have already declared themselves in favour of the issue of reparation by former European powers for the two crimes, and to participate in all events that will be held at the international level on the issue of reparation in order to make the world hear the voice of those who, after 2001, decided to make the French State pay for the crimes it committed.

MIR International will therefore give the question of reparation its global dimension and will seek to raise the awareness of all political leaders of countries that are victims of exploitation and domination by the West on this primordial question to ask the West, the question of reparation for 5 centuries of looting and violence against all dominated countries, that is to say, the crimes committed by colonialism, a system that replaced the slave trade and slavery in order to perpetuate an abusive domination of the world.

MIR International will therefore have the high task of taking over at the international level the work carried out by MIR Martinique at the national level by giving the question of reparation its true historical and global dimension.

REPARATIONS —An an urgent requirement for humanity

Reparation, a demand for justice

By Claudette Duhamel & Alain Manville

Lawyers, Vice-President and Member of the MIR

Reparation must first of all be part of a vision of liberation of thought and of men, which implies a vast enterprise of restructuring the dehumanized and enslaved human being.

It therefore postulates reparation of the human in its spiritual dimension and in its dignity as a human being.

It must be a tool at the service of the total liberation and fulfilment of the Peoples of Africa and of deported and enslaved Africans.

For the Afro-descendant Peoples of the Caribbean, reparation is therefore essential to regain the real freedom, meaning the true freedom of the spirit, having the power to express a thought that is as much as possible the fruit of an interior deliberation free from alienation.

However, for many Africans and Peoples of the Diaspora, such reparation can only be a kind of utopia, because according to them, the crimes that have been committed, that have caused such amount of suffering and pain to their people there is no way to repair them.

Such an analysis, which claims to be objective, is in reality a denial to face the reality of our peoples who are still suffering from the serious consequences of this system, which has been lasting, as far as the transatlantic trade is concerned, more than three centuries.

The backwardness of our countries' development linked to the exploitation of our human and natural resources is a direct result of the system of enslavement that the slave trade was, enslavement and colonization.

While it is true that a human being who has been deeply debased will always remember it, and in that sense any crime that violates human dignity can never be erased, there is nothing to prevent it from being repaired.

Psychologically, these peoples, entangled in contradictory approaches, are suffering and are running away form all this.

While the crimes committed can never be erased, they remain as gaping wounds in the collective memory of peoples, and must be repaired.

Europeans who today try to minimize them cannot, however, erase the stench of guilt and responsibility that led them to officially acknowledge these crimes, while continuing to adopt aggressive attitudes towards the black peoples who are the victims.

The descendants of deported Africans and Africans, while seeking to spare Europe because of their situation of economic dependence, cannot nevertheless forget that it is this same Europe that is at the root of the dramatic situation they are experiencing.

In 1985, associations were created between Martinican and Guadeloupeans, including the CIPN under the impetus of Martinican such as Me MANVILLE, and G. MALSA and the Guadeloupean LUC REINETTE and the late Batonnier RODHES.

For more than 30 years now, therefore, actions to bring about reparation have been set in **motion through various actions aimed at shattering the official collective memory which both imposes a vision of history to the glory of the colonial power and the repression of the central question of this ante and post slave history, namely the question of reparation**.

Thus, over the years, the voice of our peoples has been amplified through numerous events, including silent marches in Paris, the realization, thanks to the will of the former mayor of the commune of Sainte-Anne, of a triangular journey to restore the memory of the crime to young people and to make them aware of the need to get involved in a reparation process;

This convoy took place in 1998 between Nantes, Goree and then Martinique in Sainte-Anne. The debate was thus brought to the public arena and it is under the weight of this vast movement that France adopted in 2001 the law recognizing the slave trade and the slavery of Africans as a crime against humanity.

However, although France, forced by history to recognize the crime, was keen to ensure that this recognition did not imply reparation, it therefore only organized in this text the construction of places of memory, the inclusion of the subject of the slave trade and slavery in history books, in short, steps which, while having the merit of existing, remain ineffective in providing material compensation to the beneficiaries of the victims of these two crimes.

We have therefore made a point of letting France know through various symbolic actions, but above all through the initiation of legal proceedings that have been initiated that remind everyone of the inescapable fact that the recognition of the crime necessarily implies its material reparation. Because to refuse this principle is to continue to deny the humanity of the black man.

These actions were of a symbolic, legal and political nature.

The symbolic actions have notably resulted, since 2001, in the organization of konvwa for reparation on themes recalling the need for our peoples to pay homage to our Ancestors and honour our African roots and to renew links between the Diaspora and Africa. This has been a main focus.

Through this convoy which lasts a fortnight in May each year, we intend to make the people of Martinique understand that by anchoring themselves in their African roots, they can regain the impetus towards real freedom which consists -in the first place- in demanding respect for their human dignity.

At the political level, the MIR has participated in numerous international colloquia held in the Caribbean, the United States and Europe. On this occasion we have established lasting ties with the Caribbean by taking our place in the reparation movement launched by CARICOM.

But it is at the legal level that the MIR has launched an important battle to have the right to reparation for Afro-descendants recognized.

Since May 2005, a group of lawyers has been bringing legal proceedings before French judges to force them to condemn the French State for the two crimes of which it was one of the main perpetrators between the fifteenth and the first half of the nineteenth century.

The actions of this collective will be based on the Law of 21 May 2001 under which the Parliament of the French State, a former slaveholding power that had organized the slave trade and the enslavement of millions of Africans deported in the Caribbean Islands, voted a law acknowledging that this trade and enslavement constituted a crime against humanity.

This law reads as follows: "*the French Republic recognizes that the transatlantic slave trade and the slave trade in the Indian Ocean on the one hand and slavery on the other, perpetrated from the 15th century onwards in the Americas and the Caribbean, in the Indian Ocean and in Europe against the African, Amerindian, Malagasy and Indian populations constitutes a crime against humanity*".

This text was adopted at the instigation of many Martinican and Guadeloupean associations, such as the ICNP and the MIR.

This text gave rise to wide-ranging debates and strong resistance from many French parliamentarians who feared that the descendants of slaves would come, like the Jews, to take legal action for this crime against humanity.

The demand for reparation was therefore not mentioned in this law and the French state thought it had simply voted a so-called memorial law, i.e. without any legal consequences as to the necessary reparation of the crime against humanity.

In doing so, the French State remained in line with its doctrine applied to the populations descended from slavery, the Afrodescendants, in its last colonies, which consists quite simply in no recognition of their right to full and complete **humanity, which implies the right to reparation for crimes that undermine their dignity.**

Indeed, the crime against humanity constitutes **a denial of the inherent dignity of the human person** or of the group of persons who were victims of this crime;

Respect for human dignity must not be subject to any exception and is imposed on the authorities responsible for enforcing it, in this case French judicial authorities.

The adoption of this law would open the way for the establishment of legal action for reparation, but also for the respect of our humanity by the French constituted bodies including justice, as we shall see, is based on justice.

I - ACTIONS BEFORE A CIVIL COURT FOR REPARATION AGAINST THE FRENCH STATE THAT ORGANISED THE SLAVE TRADE AND SLAVERY

It should be noted that there are many royal edicts organizing the slave trade that the French State financed.

Moreover, the French state went so far as to codify slavery and its avatars in a terrible text, the Code Noir.

The reading of this text is edifying, and all the more terrible as it is made to believe that it was taken to prevent abuses from slave owners.

Given his role as an organizer, and also as a beneficiary of these crimes, it seemed logical to sue the criminal French state.

A first action before the civil judge was first brought by the MIR and the CMDPA (World Council of the Pan African Diaspora) in May 2005, followed by the voluntary intervention of a number of Afrodescendants.

Within the framework of this first action, a provision of 200 million euros was requested and the designation of a college of experts made up of specialists in various fields to make proposals for reparations.

Of course, the French State in the first place, claimed that it was not the perpetrator of the crime, referring to the acts and actions of some individuals and opposing the statute of limitations. Renouncing to deny its responsibility, which is clearly designated in the text of the Taubira Law, it tried to evade the judicial judge by pleading the jurisdiction of the administrative judge.

In 2008, the judge of Fort-de-France recognized the judicial jurisdiction, while alleging that the action conducted under the sign of assault posed a difficulty since the said crime was, according to him, at the time of its commission, legal as demonstrated by the Black Code.

The plaintiffs demonstrated that the Black Code, an illegal text that was applied in the colonies by a coup de force, since it had not been submitted by Colbert to "registration" by the Paris parliament as required by the law of the former regime, could not have legalized a crime.

Facing the arguments developed by the plaintiffs before the court, the Cour de cassation in criminal proceedings found a way to overcome the objections that were made to the statute of limitations and the impossibility of legally excluding from the Taubira Law the principle of material and financial reparation for the two crimes legally qualified as crimes against humanity.

In a decision handed down on February 13, 2013, the Court of Cassation in this case opposing anti-racism associations to a descendant of slavers who had made an apology for the crime against humanity to enucleate the Taubira Act, ruling that it constituted a private memory law of normative scope.

By this means, the Court of Cassation pursued only one aim, to deprive the plaintiffs' action of its main legal basis, the TAUBIRA Act, which was thus devoid of any normative scope and therefore lacking in legal efficiency, could no longer serve as a basis for a claim for reparation and could no longer stand in the way of the State's major argument that the statute of limitations was outdated.

It had to argue further that the action was time-barred, that it was the responsibility of another court that adjudicated disputes between the administration and private individuals, and finally that the slave trade and slavery were legal during the period in which it was practised, since it was not abolished until 1948.

The proceedings before the court, which lasted almost 9 years and ended with the rejection of the claims, the court finding that the claim made as the slave's heir was inadmissible because it was time-barred.

In this judgment of 29 April 2014, the court admitted that the claims of the Afro-descendants made in their personal capacity and not as beneficiaries of their ancestors were indeed admissible as not time-barred, but rejected them for lack of proof by the latter, according to the court, of a direct and certain causal relationship between the facts denounced and the alleged prejudices.

The court therefore did not deny their right to reparation as the decision of the Court of Cassation invited them to do. It simply based its decision on the statute of limitations on the action, considering that the latter, having regard to the time spent, could not justify a prejudice sufficiently linked to the crimes suffered by those of their Ancestors who had been victims of trafficking or slavery.

An appeal of this decision was filed by MIR and CMDPA and the Afro-descendant plaintiffs.

In a decision dated 19 December 2017, the Court of Appeal of Fort-de-France had to confirm the judgment, but on other grounds that paradoxically lead to the legal legitimization of the victims' claim for reparation, which was decried as the result of a legal blunder or ignorance on the part of those who led it.

The Court of Appeal held, in particular, that the statute of limitations had expired on the basis of the following argument: Afrodescendants had been able to act since the decree of 1848 abolishing slavery in Martinique, which recognized that slavery was an attack on human dignity; that if the action was suspended because of their material and moral situation until they were able to act, they did not provide proof of the impediment that would have lasted for 100 years and which would have hindered their action. It would be continued beyond that period.

The Court of Appeal, over and above the argument based on the overly late reaction of the rightful claimants, who only intervened in May 2005, i.e. more than 57 years after May

1948, endorsed the opportunistic and political jurisprudence of the Court of Cassation, according to which the imprescriptibility of crimes against humanity in French law would be valid only for the Nazi crimes judged by the Nuremberg Tribunal and would exclude all other crimes because of the non-retroactivity of criminal law in domestic law.

This jurisprudence of the Court of Cassation had been developed in the late 1980s to preserve the French State and some of its prosecutors for crimes committed in Algeria against its own jurisprudence, this time in conformity with international and domestic law, established in the Barbie and Touvier cases concerning Nazi crimes. It went so far as to challenge the imprescriptible nature of the crimes against humanity that were the slave trade and black slavery on the grounds that no text provided for a general principle of retroactivity of laws intended to prosecute and punish crimes against humanity.

However, the new argument of the Fort-de-France Court of Appeal of 2017 intended to prevent the demand for reparation was based on an error of law regarding the burden of proof, since the Court of Appeal placed the burden of proof on the plaintiffs for reparation on a fact that it was incumbent on the French State to report. Failing this, the State was to be ordered to make reparation.

Indeed, in addition to the legal fact that it was not up to the Afro-descendant claimants to prove the end of an impediment to act, the continuation of this impediment was inferred from all the official positions taken by France's highest political representatives as well as from the decision of the highest legal authority, the Court of Cassation itself, which by its ruling of 5 February 2013 had denied them any right to act after the crime had been recognized by a legislative text.

To date, it can therefore validly be considered that the impediment has not been lifted, unless there is proof to the contrary and it is impossible for the French State to provide concrete proof.

The Court of Cassation, seized of an appeal in cassation against the Fort-de-France ruling, had to apply its jurisprudence tending to deprive us of any right to reparation.

The Court of Cassation, thus seized of a priority constitutionality question (QPC) on the legality of the law, refused to refer this question to the Constitutional Council, taking the place of that court on its own initiative. It considered, as it had already done in its famous decision of 5 February 2013, that the law having no normative scope could not therefore, in addition to serving as a basis for legal action, but above all violate a constitutional principle.

This decision on QPC by the Court of Cassation is in line with the line of defense of the interests of the French State, of which the ruling handed down on February 5, 2013 was the exemplary formulation, the sole purpose of the latter having been to halt any claim for compensation on the basis of the TAUBIRA Law, which is considered to be an empty shell.

The MIR and a number of Afro-descendants took this denial of justice to the European Court of Justice in August 2019.

A second lawsuit before the civil judge was brought by the MIR and other Afro-descendants for the same purpose on the basis of the Taubira Law.

The judgment, which was handed down on 4 April 2017, is essentially based on the jurisprudence of the judgment of 5 February 2013, which ruled that the Taubira Act has no normative scope and that it cannot serve as a basis for financial reparations or any kind of reparation action for the benefit of Afro-descendants.

An appeal has been made against this judgment, reiterating the first errors of the court in 2014 and those of the Supreme Court of Appeal through the decisions of the civil courts. In response to our claims for compensation we have been able to make it clear :

- that the French State, which proclaims the equality of citizens, refuses any idea of reparation for Afro-descendants who were victims of the slave trade and slavery, even though it has recognized the principle of reparation for victims of Nazi crimes, i.e. white Jewish citizens.

- that this State refuses to apply the general principle of law that reparation should apply as soon as there is fault and injury, as it is the case with the slave trade and slavery.

- that it refuses to apply to the slave trade and slavery of Blacks the inescapable characteristic of imprescriptibility, since it rejects each time claims on the pretext that they are time-barred

- that in doing so, France's vision which is that of Europe is always to consider that there are several races and therefore that they are hierarchized in such a way that they must be treated unequally in law. Crimes against humanity committed against the Jews are imprescriptible, while those committed against Afro-descendants are time-barred and they can no longer be repaired for crimes whose consequences are still very much present.

Thus the French State, which proclaims the equality of citizens, refuses to provide for reparation in the 2001 Law on the grounds that the Taubira Law is memorial, whereas it claims that the Gayssot Law, which concerns Jewish victims of Nazi crimes, is not.

By our demands for reparation before the French courts we have forced the French State, which claims to be the homeland of human rights, to remove the mask and show the hideous face of a neo-colonialism that it applies to all the Black Peoples of the Caribbean and Africa still under its domination.

This determination not to make reparation and France's denial of humanity towards the Black People were also highlighted during the actions before the criminal courts brought by the MIR with a view to having certain descendants of slavers punished, who, being very present and powerful in Martinique, were able to make an apology for this system and for the former slavery society.

Here again, the French courts working in Martinique have protected these racists by refusing to apply the 2001 law, which qualifies the law as non-normative and therefore cannot be used as a basis for the offence of apology for crimes against humanity.

Seized by the MIR with an appeal against these discriminatory decisions, the ECHR (European Court of Human Rights) has just declared at the end of February 2020, the said appeal admissible, and a sanction by France for the failings of its civil courts is more than likely. In that it finally opens the way to the implementation of a real reparation for all Afro-descendants, this decision is historic and very important for the whole of humanity.

II ACTIONS BEFORE CRIMINAL COURTS FOR THE RESPECT OF THE DIGNITY OF AFRO-DESCENDANTS

The 2001 Law allows us to go much further in the reparation of the crimes against humanity suffered.

Thus, there is an important work of research to be done on the side of the big companies located in Martinique as well as in France to obtain that they repair whereas they built their fortune on the work of slaves.

On the basis of the 2001 law, the MIR lawyers are considering taking this route, which requires serious research and therefore has a very high cost without any measure with the current resources of this association.

The 2001 Act has already enabled us to do essential work on the consciences of Afro-descendants by attacking the doctrine that continues to allow the French state and the descendants of slaveholders to maintain the Black People in a situation of lawlessness, namely that of creolization.

The collective's work today is to exploit in multiple procedures the jurisprudence of the Court of Cassation on the impediment to act by multiplying the areas of litigation before all the French courts according to the strategy of "one, two, three, one hundred, one thousand Vietnam".

This vision of the world was implemented by Europeans, including white slaves, and applied to slaves in order to perpetuate slavery since it was absolutely necessary to make the slave accept his fate as a slave by leading him to consider himself as belonging to another species of another race than that of the white master, an inferior species since he was a slave and had no choice but to assimilate himself to the tastes of the colonist.

This thesis was widely developed by European theorists to justify slavery and to allow its perpetuation.

The belief in the existence of several races is at the root of racism, which is constituted not simply when one race is advocated as superior to another, but simply when the existence of several human species is considered to be true.

In our post-slavery world, the Creole vision continues to postulate the existence of several races and inevitably their hierarchy, which in fact justifies the unequal legal treatment applied to us.

The Taubira Law gave the opportunity to seize the repressive jurisdictions against the advocates of this Creole ideology, which obviously constitutes an apology for the crime against humanity, as we shall see. The French State understood perfectly well that it was under attack in the very legitimacy and legality of the doctrine it was imposing on us and sought through its highest court to short-circuit the effects of the 2001 Act, which made it possible, through the scope of the procedures it opened, to combat the racist theory of creolization.

In fact, on the basis of this law and other texts prohibiting the glorification of crimes against humanity, actions have been taken to convict the descendants of slaveholders who glorified slavery by promoting the creolization that was its ideological support.

In fact, in addition to the 2001 law recognising this crime, we have an arsenal of texts included in the so-called press law, which punishes the contestation and apology of crimes against humanity.

A first action was taken before the criminal court by associations fighting against racism against a descendant of a slave-driver who had allowed himself on the airwaves to make an apology for this crime against humanity.

The MIR had to file two complaints in 2010 and 2011 against a descendant of a slaver and his association called "tous créoles" for apology of crime against humanity, the latter praising creolization.

It is therefore this doctrine that was first attacked by the associations that brought Mr. HUGUES DESPOINTES before a repressive judge.

It is on the occasion of this lawsuit that the French State via its highest Court of Justice the Court of Cassation tried to cut short any lawsuit for reparation initiated, whereas in this case the Court of Appeal of Martinique had to recognize the crime of apology of crime against humanity, the highest French Court of Justice called Court of Cassation had at the end of a decision of February 5, 2013 to overturn this decision and render a decision aiming at making the Law of 2001 totally inoperative.

The Court of Cassation considered "*that if the Act of 21 May 2001 seeks to acknowledge the slave trade and slavery as a crime against humanity, such a legislative provision, whose sole purpose is to recognize an offence of this nature, cannot be covered by the normative scope of the law and characterize one of the elements constituting the crime of apology".*

In that judgment, France, through its highest court, indicated to the Afro-descendant that no action brought on the basis of the Taubira Act could prosper.

We have therefore come up against this eminently discriminatory position throughout the proceedings that have been instituted against the apologetic statements of both the descendants of slaves and the magistrates.

Indeed, faced with such a violation of our right to dignity, the MIR decided to file a complaint with the public prosecutor against the magistrates of the Court of Cassation who had issued such a decision.

These magistrates were subsequently brought before the Criminal Court of Paris, but were obviously acquitted. The repressive court had to go further since it did not follow up on the MIR's appeal, the file having been lost between the criminal court and the Paris Court.

In this complaint the MIR recalled the perfectly normative character of the law which had been the subject of several decrees, i.e. texts taken by the government for the application of the Law.

It pointed out that the Act had amended articles of law, including article 48-1 of the Act of 29 July 1881 on freedom of the press, by inserting after the words: "*by its statutes, to*" the words: "*defend the memory of slaves and the honour of their descendants*".

It was clear that the decision of the Court of Cassation was a decision of a political nature intended to render ineffective all proceedings brought before both civil and criminal courts for compensation or against the statements of the descendants of slaves and their supporters.

The repressive courts should initially feel comforted by the jurisprudence of 5 February in rejecting all actions brought on the basis of the Taubira Law for apology of the crime against humanity.

Thus, on another complaint filed by the MIR with the Investigating Judge of Fort-de-France for apology for a crime against humanity against a descendant of a slaver who had promoted the Creole system, the judge based himself on this decision of the Court of Cassation of 5 February 2013 not to prosecute the latter before the court.

On appeal by the MIR, the Court of Appeal upheld this decision by issuing a most racist decision since it referred to races and even human "strains".

The MIR had to bring all these magistrates before repressive courts, considering that they in turn were making an apology for the crime against humanity and were flouting all French texts against discrimination, based on their Creole and hence racist conception of the world, since they had a pluralist vision of humanity according to which there are several human natures, which led them to deny that the dignity of the victims of Black slavery was equal to that of the victims of the Second World War.

Of course, our actions were unsuccessful, but they did have a certain modest impact, since the second complaint against the same descendant of a slaver was not treated in the same way, since the judge in charge of the investigation decided to refer him to the criminal court.

What should be remembered is that since these different procedures, no repressive judge in Martinique has relied on this decision of February 5, 2013 to refuse to prosecute for apology of crime against humanity when we act on the basis of the Law of 2001.

It is finally only the civil court which in its judgment of April 4, 2017 had to decide to apply this jurisprudence in the second reparation procedure.

However, one thing must be noted: all the legal actions of the MIR are likely to make Afro-descendants aware of the non-recognition by the French State of their fundamental right to dignity, since by obstinately refusing to recognize their right to reparation, this State does not hesitate to go outside the law with regard to its own legislation.

This awareness will enable us to understand that it is now up to us to promote genuine solidarity between all Afro-descendants in order to form a powerful common front to break the bonds of domination.

February 22, 2020

REPARATIONS —An an urgent requirement for humanity

For an international tribunal for reparation: the ICTR

By Alain Manville

Lawyer and member of the MIR

"The problem of the 20th century is the problem of the color line." This is Du Bois's fundamental intuition.

The problem of the 21st century will be the problem of repair.

Susan SONTAG had the lucidity and the courage to say the historical essence of our time. In the words of a violent but ruthlessly true truth: *"The white race is the cancer of human history".*

These words, which tell a truth that few want to face up to, apply to Europe, the Europe of which she could also write *"that she was responsible for the greatest catastrophes of Humanity".*

This deadly quality of Europe is rooted in its ontological inability to see the other as one and the same, as a self, leading it to reduce him or her to the element of wilderness, an infinite field for the expansion of its will to power.

Globalization, or more precisely the will to globalize that carries the West and its dominant ideology, is the product of this inability to think of the other, to escape from the logic of a one-dimensional and totalitarian thought where everything is reducible to a single universality, a point which is a pure optical illusion, that based on the oblivion of the multiplicity of perspectives, the reign of the single thought, but also of the dictatorship of the one, the one that the West defines in an exclusive and undivided manner.

With this beginning of the 21st century, things have changed, from a shift that was already announced since the fall of the Berlin Wall, the end of Marxist ideologies, the rise of new economic poles in the world, China, India and Brazil, and far behind Africa, shivering but paralysed by the former colonial powers, first and foremost France, with the accentuated pursuit of Françafrique.

Civilizational decline of the West, shifting lines of force, readjustment of balances, emergence of new situations, modification of the configuration of the world and the impasse of the political and social systems set up by the West, of which Europe is bearing the brunt more and more acutely.

It is in this context, which has been modified for more than 30 years, that a demand that had hitherto been stifled by the noise of the world, a world focused on questions of independence, on North/South relations, on the global management of economic crises, on the narcissism of nation states and their narrow egoism, has emerged with force, namely the demand for reparation: Reparation by the West of all the crimes that are at the basis of its historical success, of its takeover of world domination and of its claim to be the culmination of a history whose completion it would accomplish, setting for Humanity the golden age of its system of meaning and value.

The movement for the reparation of the crimes of the slave trade and slavery has shown the way in demanding far-reaching changes.

The reparation of the victims of the two crimes of trafficking and slavery and their beneficiaries, something that is a priori obvious, is still being challenged and rooted in positions that have never been questioned;

Both a large part of jurists and public opinion think that the question of reparation is a non-issue and, in any case is really an ideology of dissent from the common values of the republic and, constitutes a dangerous challenge to living together philosophy.

Raising the issue of material reparation for the two crimes would be a matter for a regime that is a victim of memory that would get bogged down in an anti-republican ideology.

As Johann Michel points it out, the official ideology in fact contains the question of recognition of the two crimes in a commemoration speech based on the idea of the irreparable nature of the crime, at least for the victims of the crime, the slavers having been refunded.

"In spite of nuances that we cannot dwell on here, it must be acknowledged that official commemorations, from one end of the political spectrum to the other, honour above all the greatness of the Abolitionist Republic and the personality of Victor Schoelcher... Little will be said about the black

liberators, the runaways or the victims of colonial slavery who were largely banned from official celebrations. The recognition of slavery as a crime against humanity and the question of possible moral or financial reparations are not part of the "framing of memory policies in this 1998 year, the main characteristic of the republican abolitionist memorial regime is to celebrate above all, the work of the Republic in the process of abolition. "Slavery and Reparations". Construction d'un problème public (Building a public issue 1998-2001)" Johann Michel, in Politique africaine (African policy) 2017/2 (No. 146), pages 143 to 164.

In the legal field, the thesis is that the problem of reparation as a question of law is a contradictory and comes up against a double obstacle: the desire to ignore the fact that the irreparable cannot be repaired and the fact that it is a political and moral issue having nothing to do with law.

G. Garapon's book, "*Can history be repaired ?*" Ed. Odile Jacob is the analogy of this conception of things which, taken to the extreme, lead to a negationism not only as regards to the right of victims to reparation, but also to a negationism of the criminal essence of the crime against humanity as regards slave trade and slavery.

Yet this denial of the legal nature of the issue of the right to reparation, which has become the vulgate of the republic ideologues, has been denied after more than 14 years of a large legal battle in which the French State was brought before French judges with a view to being condemned to make reparation, make reparation in the name of its duty to remember and make material and financial reparation.

After the judges had put forward a number of pleas in law, the main purpose of which was to demonstrate that there could not reasonably be a judicial remedy to obtain legal compensation for the harmful consequences of the two crimes (mainly invoking the statute of limitations and the lack of normative scope of the Taubira Act, a law excluding in any event the principle of reparation for the two crimes), the Court of Appeal decided to order the French State to make reparation for the material and financial damage caused by the two crimes, in the name of its duty of memory.

It dismissed the appellants on the ground that although the limitation period had been suspended, the appellants had acted late.

This decision was upheld by the Court of Cassation, which reiterated the grounds on which it was based, establishing a body of case law which decisive legal significance is that there is indeed a right to see the two crimes repaired, that the action for reparation has had the limitation period for that right suspended and that, in the end, once proof is adduced that the suspension of the limitation period continued beyond 1948, the claimants for reparation would not only be admissible, but would be well-founded in their claim.

In an unexpected turn of events, the Court of Cassation found and ruled as follows:

"And whereas, after stating that the Act of 21 May 2001 had not weakened these principles and that an action based on article 1382, now article 1240 of the Civil Code, of a nature to engage the responsibility of the State independently of any criminal classification of the facts, was subject both to the statute of limitations of former article 2262 of the same Code and to the forfeiture of claims against the State provided for in article 9 of the Act of 29 January 1831, which became Article 1 of the Law of 31 December 1968, the Court of Appeal decided exactly that this action, in so far as it related to facts which ended in 1848 and despite the suspension of the statute of limitations until the day on which the victims, or their heirs, were able to act, was time-barred in the absence of proof of an impediment which would have lasted for more than one hundred years.

Hence it follows that the plea is unfounded."

The Supreme Court, which from the beginning of proceedings instituted in May 2005 ensured that the applicants' action, which was based primarily on the TAUBIRA Act, was deprived of its basis, thus ruling in a parallel proceeding concerning the crime of apology for the crime against humanity that the TAUBIRA Act was a memorial law and as such deprived of normative scope, establishes a principle of action for the future.

By validating the grounds used in the Fort-de-France Court of Appeal's decision to dismiss the claimants'action for compensation, the Supreme Court opened, without its knowledge and as if by the effect of an ultimate trick of reason, the way to new proceedings for compensation, based on the 1848 decree of abolition and the demonstration that the limitation period had continued to be suspended until the present day, excluding any principle of limitation from the right to compensation for the two crimes.

Consequently, in the more or less short term, a French court will have to rule that the action for compensation of the beneficiaries, victims of the two crimes, is admissible and well-founded and to order the French State to pay compensation.

Actually, France was not the only European power to practice slavery, and although it played a key role among European nations, it was not the only one to deport and enslave negroes.

England, Holland, Spain, Portugal, the United States, Sweden, Denmark, Belgium, all of them practised the triangular trade and enslavement of Africans.

The French judge does not have jurisdiction to judge these States, which, like the French State, owe reparation to the victims of the two crimes and their heirs.

Although, notwithstanding the position taken by the Court of Cassation, French law, thanks to the TAUBIRA Act, allows French judges to bring claims for reparation before French courts, this is not the situation for most of the former slave nations, which have always refused to receive in their domestic law such legal recognition of the crime against humanity of their past slavery practices.

Indeed, the legal recognition of the crime against humanity of the slave trade and slavery under the TAUBIRA Act provides the principle for the indictment of all these former slave powers.

The law allows it, but the court to judge it is lacking.

At the end of the Second World War, the international community became aware of the need for crimes against humanity and genocide to be prosecuted against those responsible for these crimes;

It was established at the institution of the Nuremberg Tribunal by the victorious Allied forces of Nazi Germany a series of international tribunals to judge crimes against humanity committed in the world.

The Criminal Tribunals for Rwanda, Cambodia and the former Yugoslavia were the instruments set up by the international community to judge those responsible for the massacres of populations that were crimes against humanity or genocide.

It is clear that the European States which took the initiative in setting up these ad hoc tribunals were cautious enough at the Durban conference in February 2001 to oppose the vote on a resolution aimed at having the slave trade and slavery recognized in international law as a crime against humanity and the principle of reparation.

Mr. Beckles in his book "BRITAIN's black' debt" relates the bitter struggle of Western countries to ensure that such a resolution would never appear in the conference final resolutions and would not serve as a legal basis for possible indictment of these States, all of which participated in the commission of the two crimes from the 15th to the end of the 19th century.

Although the legal obstacle has been removed in France, and today with the Supreme Court's decision, the path of reparation proceedings is open to all those who are entitled to the victims of the two crimes and who are able to provide proof that the impediment to act, which continued until April 1948, has continued until today, the absence of an international jurisdiction to judge these two crimes covered by the imprescriptibility of crimes against humanity constitutes an obstacle to implicating all the former slave powers and obtaining their condemnation to repair the harmful consequences of the two crimes.

Before the French judge, on the basis of the legal recognition of the two crimes as crimes against humanity voted by the French parliament, the victims' beneficiaries had requested two things: a provision for future reparation and an assessment of the harmful consequences of the two crimes in order to set the amount of this reparation.

Before an international tribunal for reparation, such actions become possible.

It is therefore necessary to find African States willing to establish such a tribunal on the model of the ad hoc international tribunals that the United Nations is setting up with the task of organizing the trial of European States with a view to reparation for the harmful consequences of their responsibility in the commission of these two crimes.

However, the idea seems to have run up against an insurmountable obstacle, that of an agreement by the majority of nations, members of the UN, the institution within which former slave powers have granted themselves the exorbitant privilege of a right of veto, an indication and sign of their domination over the world and the protection of their particular interests to the detriment of those of the League of Nations.

This right of veto is the result of a history that is not unrelated to the existence of the two crimes and to the commission of these crimes by these nations endowed with this privilege.

Behind the apparent facade of a democratic institution where all nations would be equally represented stands a tool of Western domination over other nations.

This situation is the result of a historically established balance of power which reflects the racist ideology of the superiority of the white man, which has been rooted in the European consciousness since the fifteenth century and which was one of the major vectors of the slave trade and slavery.

At that time, the West was established as the expression of a superior civilization made up of peoples whose vocation was to dominate the world and make it the field of its exploitation.

As G Mairet reminds us in his book "la fable du monde":

"The morality of modern States begins and is consolidated with the project of the Europeans to use their domination over the wilderness of the ewe and to make the area thus discovered and the populations living there, the territory of their sovereignty. In so doing, they transfigured the ewe into the world and founded the morality of modern times. What is called civilization is this process of civilizing the expanse, the passage from the wilderness to the world, the transformation of the savage into the civilized, of the small tribes into a nation. The Wilderness, a wild and deserted expanse, is not without inhabitants; on the contrary, it is inhabited, but for the conquerors, the peoples who live there are themselves part of the Wilderness, they are only a modality of resextensa. The philosophy of the moderns in describing their condition as that of life in the state of nature produces the concept of the aborigine considered from the point of view of civilized Europe' " p 131 edition NRF essays

This representation of the world is inseparable from the advent of the mass deportation of negroes and their enslavement; it is based on a delusional idea of the supremacy of the white man, an idea that was by no means abolished with the abolition of slavery, but remained in the heart of Western thought and of all institutions through colonialism and the "*elaboration of the Kantian idea of the League of Nations at the political level, the first political manifestation of which was the establishment of the*

61

"League of Nations" at the end of the catastrophe of the First World War. " Max Hubert in his book *"le bon samaritain"* (Paris la Baconnière 1943, P 43) could note :

"This conception of civilization typical of the humanitarist spirit must be understood in a wider context. Indeed, this conception runs through the whole of Western modernity, with a strong dose of ethnocentrism. The authors of the Enlightenment in particular contributed to its expression. In this perspective, one can also consider that the reactionary thoughts following the French Revolution are part of a common background of ideas common to the socialist theories that developed in parallel. Both are in fact traversed by the certainty of Europe's superiority over the rest of the world, from the point of view of civilization, but also of race. At the beginning of the nineteenth century, Saint-Simon envisioned a European confederation to which he assigned very significant purposes: "The surest way to maintain peace in the confederation will be to carry it constantly out of itself, and to occupy it unceasingly with great internal works. To populate the globe with the European race, which is superior to all other races of men, and make it possible for them to travel and live in (the globe) like in Europe... "

This problem of the superiority of the white man is readable within the legal constitution of this new order wanted by the main Western powers of the time, France, England, and the USA.

This representation of the superiority of the white man transpires even in the texts of international law promoting the concept of the "*League of Nations*", which is supposed to recognize the equality of all human beings and their shared rights to protection of the community of these nations united as guarantors of the respect due to the human rights that it establishes as a supreme principle.

The article 22 of the Covenant of the League of Nations, which determines the modalities of the organization's assignments, makes this clear:

"*Following principles shall apply to colonies and territories which, as a result of war, have ceased to be under the sovereignty of the States which previously governed them and which are **inhabited by peoples not yet able to govern themselves in the particularly difficult conditions of the modern world**. The well-being and development of these peoples constitute a sacred mission of civilization, and it is appropriate to incorporate in the present Covenant guarantees for the accomplishment of this mission. The best method of practically realizing this principle is **to entrust the trusteeship of these peoples to those developed nations which, by reason of their resources, experience or geographical position, are best able to assume this responsibility** and which are willing to accept it: they would exercise this trusteeship as Agents and on behalf of the Society.* "

This process of domination has come to an end and, as Michel Onfray reminds us, we have entered the phase of decadence and twilight of the white world's domination over the other non-white peoples; the face of the world is changing.

In this fundamental change where all the landmarks are going to change, where the old evidence is going to collapse, where the certainties that have kept the world standing (and lying down for those on the other side) for 5 centuries are unravelling and where new spiritual gifts are taking shape, inheriting the achievements of_Western rationality, but refusing to submit henceforth to the dictatorship of its prejudices, a new world order is being forged.

It should thus be noted that the West's power of influence was still strong at the 2001 Durban conference, where African heads of state made the unthinkable alliance with Western countries to oppose the question of reparation being one of the issues calling for decisions to be taken by the speakers.

As Hilary Beckles reminds us, Europeans, following Americans, found a way to remove the issue of reparation from the issues leading to a resolution.

International forces and power relations are irretrievably reorganizing and there are emerging new powers that will eventually blow up the system of this more than five-centuries old white world domination.

In this context, the point of reparation for the crimes committed by the West and the fierce exploitation imposed on the whole world, finally unlocked from the powerful censorship of Western powers for almost half a century, will come to be raised as a historical issue.

Africa, which has been the major victim of this desire for domination and negation of the other which has led to the genocide of several peoples (in South America the Aztec and Inca peoples, in North America the Indians of the first nations), is witnessing this shift in white supremacy of which South Africa was the last model, declaring this regime of total enslavement of the other which the European powers have continued to practice in the name of their world order and so-called democratic values.

The issue of reparation will be the major issue of the 21st century, and first and foremost that of the crimes of trafficking and slavery.

In this context of the decline and weakening of the dictatorship that Westerners have imposed on the world for five centuries, it is possible to finally raise the question of reparation for these two major crimes against humanity that have been the result of the globalization of the world.

The project of establishing an international criminal court for reparation and its promotion by one or more African states brave enough to take the risk of a violent opposition from former slave powers, is therefore on the UN agenda and the establishment of such a court of justice is an unavoidable fact to come.

It will be the initiator of a process in which all peoples and nations that have been the victims of the predatory actions of the West will be able to claim reparation from all those States that have built the good life of one part of the world based on the absolute misery of its other.

It has now been established that the question of reparation for the two crimes of the slave trade and slavery is indeed a legal issue founded on the system of international law and which meets the requirements of justice of the different systems of law of the former slave powers.

When Africa regains the majority that the Western powers have stolen from it and asserts itself as a world that claims its true autonomy and self-determination, then the court of reparation will do its work and justice will ultimately be done to those millions of men, women and children who were crushed by the death drive that animated and continues to animate these deadly powers and their delusional will to power.

The European Slave Trade, African Resistance and the Question of Reparations: Towards an Objective Assessment of the Damage Suffered by the Victims of the Black Holocaust and their Descendants

By Pr Coovi Rekhmiré

Egyptologist, Philosopher and Historian.

Specialist of the European Negro Trafficking

To my Dean Garcin Malsa, the "Justicier de Maät" who opened the way for us to rehabilitate the memory of the Black Holocaust Deportees.

Quote from the "NEGRE FONDAMENTAL" Aimé Césaire.

"Let us imagine Auschwitz and Dachau, Ravensbrück and Mathausen, but all on an immense scale - that of the centuries, that of the continents - America transformed into a concentration camp universe, the striped uniform imposed on a whole race, the word given sovereignly to the kapos and the schlague, a gloomy lament criss-crossing the Atlantic, piles of corpses at every stop in the desert or the forest, and the petty bourgeois from Spain, England, France, Holland, innocent Himmler of the system, amassing from all this the hideous loot, the criminal capital that will make them leaders of industry. Let us imagine all this, and all the spittle of history and all the humiliations and all the

sadisms, and let us add them up and multiply them, and we will understand that Nazi Germany only applied in small measure to Europe what Western Europe applied for centuries to the races that had the audacity or the awkwardness to stand in its way. The admirable thing is that the Negro held out. Many died. The others held on. How could they? Because of the Negro kindness that made one man strengthen the other. Because of the Negro imagination that always presented them with freedom within reach. Because of their love for life, and the Negro liveliness that made them superior to their condition and always judging their masters. The fact is that they did not sink into complete decline, they never lost hope, they never gave up their dignity and that went on and on, day after day, for two centuries, they kept plotting, apparently resigned, never tamed ".

cf. Aimé CÉSAIRE "*Preface*" to "*ESCLAVAGE ET COLONISATION*" by Victor SCHŒLCHER, page 18.

Of all the crimes perpetrated by human beings against other human beings since the world has been a world, the EUROPEAN SLAVE TRADE (tragic episode of BLACK HOLOCAUST () was undoubtedly the most abominable, the most unspeakable, the most abject and the most repugnant. European Nations (Spain, Portugal, England, France, Holland, etc.) which were part of this GENOCIDAL COMPANY and have been making extraordinary and colossal profit during five centuries and that made possible their INDUSTRIALIZATION ACCELERATED, are still trying, just before our eyes, to rewrite the history of this centuries-old criminal epic by insisting to make us believe that their victims are actually their executioners. Nowadays, Philip D. CURTIN's book "THE ATLANTIC SLAVE TRADE: A CENSUS" is the breviary of this pseudo-scientifically proven negationist in its most cynical form.

To this vulgate should be added a text by the same author entitled: "THE RISE AND FALL OF THE PLANTATION COMPLEX: ESSAYS IN ATLANTIC HISTORY". In France, Olivier PETRE GRENOUILLEAU has made headlines by proposing an ambivalent and incomplete "*historical synthesis*" which is, after all, only a poor and quite pathetic copy of the above-mentioned works of Philip CURTIN under the pompous title: "LES TRAITES NÉGRIÈRES : ESSAI D'HISTOIRE GLOBALE" (THE SLAVE TRADE : A GLOBAL HISTORY ESSAY). That was all it took to revive in the self-proclaimed "HUMAN RIGHTS HERITAGE" an OUTRAGEOUS DENIAL maintained since the "ENLIGHTENMENT" (we should rather say the "DARK LIGHTS CENTURY") by a militant "LOBBY ANTI-NIGGER" whose aim has always been to deny not only the extent of the inexpiable crime, but also to insinuate that it was a "LUCRATIVE AND FREELY CONSENTED TRADING THAT BENEFITTED BOTH EUROPEANS AND AFRICAN PEOPLE " (cf. HISTORY HANDBOOK OF THE 6th CLASS EDITED BY NATHAN in 1996 AND STILL INCLUDED IN THE SCHOOL PROGRAMME IN GUYANA IN 2016). The work of Olivier PETRE GRENOUILLEAU has received, as was to be expected, the implicit support of African researchers under "Africanist" tutelage such as Elikia M'BOKOLO, Issiaka MANDE, Ibrahima THIOUB, Pape

N'DIAYE to which must be added a woman of colonist descent coming from the over-mediatized Reunion Island such as Françoise VERGES who was promoted a few years ago by the "*fait du Prince*" President of the "COMMITTEE FOR THE MEMORY OF SLAVERY". Even the President of the French Republic, François HOLLANDE, who had recently publicly opposed the request for REPAIRS formulated for the first time to our knowledge by an eminent descendant of deported Africans like Garcin MALSA from the "MOUVEMENT INTERNATIONAL DES RÉPARATIONS" (MIR), felt that he couldn't but use part of a very explicit quote from Aimé CESAIRE to justify his cowardice. It is in the extension of this forfeiture that we consider quite appropriate to include the last two loathsome initiatives taken a year ago by the French authorities who decided before and during their "CARNIVAL CEREMONY" of Tuesday, May 10, 2016 in the GARDEN OF LUXEMBOURG by using their "HOUSE NIGGERS", to desecrate the GLORIOUS AND IMPERISSABLE MEMORY of our African Ancestors deported for five centuries to the "NEW WORLD" by the EUROPEAN STATES with the guarantee and anointing of the CATHOLIC CHURCH, APOSTOLIC AND ROMAN .

1- In an "INAUGURAL LESSON" pronounced from the top of his "CHAIR OF ARTISTIC CREATION" on March 17, 2016 at 18:00 under the intriguing title "BLACK LETTERS : FROM THE DARKNESS TO THE LIGHT", Alain MABANCKOU, a burlesque "novelist", gnawed by the "POLYVALENCE DELIRIUM", has spread his nauseating remarks on the "TRANSATLANTIC SLAVE TRADE" obviously without taking the trouble to consult any archive on the subject.

After insinuating that his communication aims above all at promoting "AFRICAN FRANCOPHONE LITERATURE" (sic), he displayed his complex moods and love afflictions towards his "Masters" while showing self-flagellation, an exercise in which he excels better than anyone else. The whole program of RECOLONIZATION OF THE IMAGINATION OF THE FRENCH NIGGERS declined on all tones by Alain MABANCKOU had already been summarized in the "MANIFESTO FOR A WORLD LITERATURE IN FRENCH" of which he was one of the forty-four signatories. About his "EARLY ATTRACTIVENESS" for the language of Molière, which the late academician Léopold Sédar SENGHOR himself would not have disavowed, Alain MABANCKOU wrote:

"At the age of 6, I discovered "words" in the French language"... Had it not been for the guarantee brought in his "INAUGURAL LESSON" too spicy to my taste to the AMBIENT NEGATING RENGAINE, Alain MABANCKOU's eclectic and erratic prose would hardly deserve a mention in our framework.

2- In a quite unusual "PRESS RELEASE" published on Monday, April 25, 2016 and opportunely entitled: "FOR A MEMORY OF COLONIAL SLAVERY THAT GATHERED THE FRENCH !" Serge ROMANA, on behalf of the "COMMITTEE MARCH OF MAY 23, 1998 (CM98)" working in collaboration with Marie-Claire FAIVRE, Vice-President of

"THE ROAD OF ABOLITIONS OF SLAVERY AND HUMAN RIGHTS" stated that she wanted the OFFICIAL COMMEMORATION to be registered under the sign of the "SHARED AND EASED MEMORY" between the descendants of the victims and those of their executioners.

This CONCERTED MEMORIAL ACTION is supposed to take place in three main phases according to the "ROAD MAP" of the two incumbents:

I - *"Together we will pay tribute to the French abolitionists by laying a wreath of flowers on the tomb of Victor SCHŒLCHER, a relentless fighter against the definitive abolition of slavery in 1848, at the Pantheon, at 10 a.m. on 27 April 2016, the 168th anniversary of the signing of the decree of the abolition of colonial slavery in French colonies.*

II- We will be standing together during the national events of May 10, 2016 on the one hand at the "Forêt Mémoire" site in Chamblanc, at the "Maison de la Négritude" in Champagney, at the "Musée Abbé Grégoire" in Emberménil, at the "Musée Victor Schœlcher" in Fessenheim and at the "Fort de Joux-Toussaint Louverture" in "Pontarlier" as well as at the national ceremony that will be taking place in the Jardin du Luxembourg in Paris.

III- Finally, we will commemorate together on 23rd May 2016 the victims of colonial slavery in departmental republican ceremonies in Saint-Denis, Sarcelles, Grigny and Creil, in religious ceremonies in the basilicas of Saint-Denis and Créteil and in the national ceremony Limyè ba Yo -

Recognition - Reconciliation which will take place due to the state of emergency, in the gardens of the Ministry of Overseas Territories".

Of the above, it appears that the French authorities are fully committed to impose their new conceptual idea of "SHARED AND EASED MEMORY" on the descendants of the African victims of a "CRIME AGAINST HUMANITY", which they also claim never to want to repair, they have commanded their "SERVING NIGGERS": Alain MABANCKOU from his chair at the "COLLÈGE DE FRANCE" and Serge ROMANA from his "JARDINS DU MINISTÈRE DE L'OUTRE-" (Gardens of the Ministry of the OUTREACH). MER" - "State of Emergency" - to accomplish the crime of self-violation of the memory of our African Ancestors deported for five centuries by the European Nations, including by this same negationist France, negrophobic and arrogant with whom they say they want to embrace under the double seal of RECOGNITION and RECONCILIATION. Convinced for our part that only HISTORICAL TRUTH and FAIR JUSTICE are the necessary prerequisites for any possible understanding between peoples who are opposed by such a serious HISTORICAL LITIGATION, we will develop during our COMMEMORATIVE CONFERENCE on Sunday, May 8, 2016 the two following "HARD POINTS":

A- The "EUROPEAN SLAVE TRADE" which began in 1444 (15th century), i.e. long before the violent conquest and destruction of the "natives" of the Continent perfidiously called "AMERICA" and which lasted until 1890 (19th century) was in fact a succession of "RAZZIAS AGAINST BLACK PEOPLE" which transformed the African Continent into an immense "TERRITORY OF ROUGH HUNTING" for the European traffickers of human flesh. In order to achieve their mercantile ends, these greedy and shady hords did not hesitate to torture, mutilate, rape, pillage, defile and degrade anything that looked like a black-skinned human being. They used and abused for firearms and the refined techniques of psychological degradation listed in Willy LYNCH's nomenclature. In his famous "TREATY OF PERFECT TRADER" hardly ever mentioned nowadays, SAVARY recalls on and on ad nauseam the "REFINED PROCESSES OF PHYSICAL AND PSYCHICAL DESTRUCTION OF NIGGERS" which constituted the very substance of the "SLAVEOWNERS LOG" carefully concealed in the reserves of the Specializing Libraries. This "APOCALYPTIC CRIME", to use DUNBAR's expression, has taken from Africa 200 million good shaped human beings at the very least, and not 15 million as Philip CURTIN and his disciples kept claiming until not so long ago. In order to re-establish at last the HISTORICAL TRUTH on this and so many other points, the great Nigerian historian Joseph INIKORI - undoubtedly the most eminent contemporary specialist on the "TRANSATLANTIC SLAVE TRADE" - and his collaborators have totally destroyed the ideological scaffolding of ACADEMIC NEGATIONISM in the monumental work entitled : "THE ATLANTIC SLAVE TRADE: EFFECTS ON ECONOMIES, SOCIETIES AND PEOPLES IN AFRICA, THE AMERICAS AND EUROPE". In another no less masterly publication, he showed the unquestionable DIALECTIC LINK between England's irresistible industrial rise and its status as a "Slave Power". He succeeded in elucidating by ricochet the correlative impoverishment of African Kingdoms and Empires that were demographically decimated and economically plundered by the Slave Trade. This was notably the case of the Ashanti Confederation in Ghana and the Edo Kingdom of Benin in Nigeria. In addition to his works, which are totally unknown in France where it is customary to quibble about the "Hollywood fictions" of PETRE GRENOUILLEAU, we can mention the essential work of Eric WILLIAMS "CAPITALISM AND SLAVERY" which remains astonishingly topical. Finally, let us mention as an indication the classic essay of the genius Walter RODNEY "HOW EUROPE UNDERDEVELOPED AFRICA" not to mention his famous article: "AFRICAN SLAVERY AND OTHER FORMS OF SOCIAL OPPRESSION ON THE UPPER GUINEA COAST IN THE CONTEXT OF THE ATLANTIC SLAVE TRADE" published in 1966 in "JOURNAL OF AFRICAN HISTORY". The major issue of all these major but little known works of the African historiography of the transatlantic slave trade is the reconstruction on a strict scientifically-based research on the "GLOBAL PROCESS OF THE DESTRUCTION OF AFRICAN CIVILIZATIONS THROUGH THE COALITION OF EUROPEAN NATIONS" as suggested by the brilliant scholar Chancellor WILLIAMS in his masterpiece "THE DESTRUCTION OF THE BLACK CIVILIZATIONS". Finally, it is important to retrace, link by link, the entire COMMAND CHAIN of the main actors of the EUROPEAN SLAVE TRADE, in accordance with the THEORY of "HISTORICAL

CAUSALITY", which is the only way to identify without passion those RESPONSIBLE for each and every one of them in this appalling tragedy.

B- Negationist historians (CURTIN, PETRE GRENOUILLEAU) willingly underreport in their targeted monographs, the HEROIC RESISTANCES opposed by the African People to the EUROPEAN SLAVE TRADE. They usually substitute them with the "SPORADIC UPRISINGS" which would be in their eyes only the sum of the spontaneous reactions of the "slaves" to the ill-treatment inflicted by zealous and clumsy traders. The height of cynicism is that some NEGATIONNISTS nowadays shamelessly criticize the rigorous work of Louis SALA MOLINS devoted to the "CODE NOIR" of 1685 edited by Minister COLBERT under the aegis of the King of France LOUIS XIV (cf. Louis SALA MOLINS "LE CODE NOIR OU LE CALVAIRE DE CANAAN "). They readily see in this monstruous text "A BOLD ATTEMPT FOR ITS TIME AIMING TO REGULATE AND HUMANIZE SLAVERY". Thus, since the publication of Olivier PETRE GRENOUILLEAU's negationist book, we have been witnessing a real media offensive aimed at imposing everywhere and in all minds the idea that there have been three "SLAVE TRADES": the "INTERNAL AFRICAN SLAVERY", the "EASTERN ARAB SLAVE TRADE" and the "TRANSATLANTIC EUROPEAN SLAVE TRADE".

The latter was finally interrupted, according to the denialist ideologues, thanks to humanitarian initiatives of the English and French EUROPEAN ABOLITIONIST LEADING

FIGURES in particular. In France, official commemorations focus exclusively on the alledged role of Abbé GRÉGOIRE and Victor SCHŒLCHER in the abolition of black slavery and when the epic of TOUSSAINT LOUVERTURE is mentioned, the explanation given is that happened sometimes by the influence of the "enlightened" ideas of the "PHILOSOPHY OF ENLIGHTMENT", sometimes by the impact of the "FRENCH REVOLUTION" in the colonies, including Santo Domingo (cf. Pierre PLUCHON "TOUSSAINT LOUVERTURE, BLACK SON OF THE FRENCH REVOLUTION"). It can be stated without any risk of contradiction that from the 15th century to the 19th century, Africa was the theatre of an INSURRECTIONAL CONTINUUM which lasted three centuries in the European colonies of the "NEW WORLD" (America, Caribbean). These were true ANTI-SLAVERY RESISTANCES which were all without exception based on a quadruple spiritual, economic, military and even political ORGANIZATION.

We will limit ourselves to studying

1- The ANTI-LABOUR RESISTANCE of the "JAGAS in Central Africa".

2- The ANTI-LABOUR RESISTANCE of the "MOUN KAM" of the "QUILOMBO DE PALMARÈS" in the State of Pernambuco in Brazil.

3- The ANTI-LABOUR RESISTANCE of the "MOUN KAM" in Haiti.

4- The ANTI-LABOUR RESISTANCE of the "MOUN KAM" of AMISTAD in Cuba, etc.

The conclusion that can be drawn at the end of this introspection of memory is that all these RESISTANCES were inspired by AFRICA and its CIVILIZATION VALUES.

No ANTI-SLAVERY RESISTANCE worthy of the name has been organized, and even more so directed by "CREOLES", "CARIBBEANS" and "ULTRA-MARINE", but exclusively by Africans who never denied their CULTURAL IDENTITY, their SPIRITUAL VALUES and their HISTORICAL ROOTS. It is by virtue of this COMMUNITY OF ORIGIN, VALUES, SUFFERING, DESTINY that five eminent figures of descendants of African deportees, namely Anténor FIRMIN (Haiti), Bénito SYLVAIN (Haiti), Henry SYLVESTER WILLIAMS (Trinidad), Martin DELANY (United States of America), Marcus GARVEY (Jamaica) laid the foundations of the most powerful black movement of contemporary times: PANAFRICANISM OF THE PEOPLES. In accordance with the crucial resolutions of the "HAITI COLLOQUIUM" devoted by UNESCO to the "TRANSATLANTIC SLAVE TRADE", Time has come for Africans and their descendants, victims of the MOST ABOMINABLE CRIME EVER PERPETRED BY HUMAN BEINGS AGAINST OTHER HUMAN BEINGS, to set about rewriting this painful chapter in the History of Humanity themselves, so that future generations can admire and celebrate the bravery, the nobleness and stamina of the resistance fighters, who, from the depths of darkness have rekindled the flame of hope.

After so many years of humiliations and delusions, it is therefore necessary to rewrite the TRUE HISTORY OF THE EUROPEAN SLAVE TRADE AND AFRICAN RESISTANCES in the wake of the pioneering research carried out by Eric WILLIAMS, Walter RODNEY, Joseph INIKORI, etc., and to rewrite it in the light of the new knowledge and experience of the African Resistance. by emphasizing the capital role played by WOMEN ("POTOMITAN") in the collective survival of the Black People from the 15th century to the 19th century. The "FACTICE AND PROFANATORY COMMEMORATION" of 10 May, which on a non-working day gave rise to CARNIVAL EXHIBITIONS in the Luxembourg Gardens in the presence of the President of the French Republic and a few hand-picked "HOUSE NIGGERS", must be abandoned. For us, May 10th is a DATE OF PROFANATION which must stop giving rise to endless gesticulations. The only HISTORICALLY JUSTIFIED AND RIGHTFUL date is August 22nd because it refers to the SPIRITUAL REGENERATION CEREMONY OF THE "BWA KAY MOUN" which was the prelude to the GENERAL INSURRECTION OF THE "MOUN KAM" under the direction of the HOUGAN BOUKMAN DUTTY. All Africans and Afro-descendants must appropriate this HIGHLY SYMBOLIC AND SACRED DATE which echoes the HEROIC RESISTANCES of our valiant and glorious Ancestors.

REPARATIONS —An an urgent requirement for humanity

An account of "Britain's Black Debt - Reparations for Caribbean Slavery and Native Genocide" by Hilary Beckles, a rewriting of history for restorative social transformation.

By Rodolphe Solbiac

Lecturer, habilitated to supervise research

English Caribbean Studies - University of the West Indies

References

1 **Hilary Beckles, Britain's Black Debt**: Reparations for Caribbean Slavery and Native Genocide (Kingston : The University of the West Indies Press, 2013), 248p, ISBN: 9789766403492.

2 **Professor Sir Hilary Beckles** is Historian, Vice-Chancellor of the University of the West Indies, Chairman of the CARICOM Reparations Committee, Vice-Chairman of the International Working Group for the UNESCO Slave Route Project.

3 **This text was published in the Journal Caribbean Studies** [Online], 31-32 | August-December 2015, online December 15, 2015.

URL http://journals.openedition.org/etudescaribeennes/7637

Reading report

Britain's Black Debt: Reparations for Caribbean Slavery and Native Genocide, published in 2013 by Professor Hilary Beckles, released at University of the West Indies Press, presents an approach to the history of British colonialism, the slave trade and the enslavement of Africans from the perspective of the damage they caused to African and indigenous Caribbean peoples and the benefits they brought to Great Britain.

The book is based on a study of the history of the slave trade in the West Indies, which was published by Professor Hilary Beckles at the University of the West Indies Press in 2013.

Beckles' unique approach in this book sets out to demonstrate the criminal nature of the African slave trade and slavery, to establish its highly lucrative nature, to identify its beneficiaries and to demonstrate the continuity between the establishment of this system in modern times and the situation in Caribbean societies today. It aims to establish the legitimacy of the action for reparations in Caribbean societies carried out since the 1990s by transnational citizen organizations, which has been entering an institutional phase since the beginning of the decade with the involvement of the University of the West Indies and CARICOM.

This book is organized in two parts with eleven and four chapters respectively. The first part presents the principles and practices of reparation before setting out the historical elements that establish the Kalinago genocide, as well as the criminal nature of the slave trade and the enslavement of Africans in the Caribbean and the Americas. It also develops the idea of the genocidal effect of this trade on Africa. The second part is devoted to the action for reparations carried out by Caribbean people and African people.

In the first part, Hilary Beckles describes the process of building the legal status that makes the African a moveable asset, a part of the heritage of a plantation that can even be used as an asset for the plantation itself that you can even rent for sexual services.

It describes how the wealth derived from the slave trade and slavery contributed economically to the building of pre-industrial and industrial British society. It highlights, for example, the benefits that the Church of England derived from this system as well as its moral contribution to the establishment of slavery as a cause of national interest. In addition to his role as a buyer, his legitimization of the fact that members of his clergy owned slaves and engaged in the trade, Beckles emphasizes the large-scale ideological and racial action of dehumanization of the African carried out by this religious institution. He points to the considerable damage to the mental health and self-esteem of black people that can still be seen throughout the post-plantationary world.

In addition to the church, the role of the political class and the aristocracy are analyzed to demonstrate the involvement of all sectors of English society in the organization of crime against Africans. Thus, Britain's Black Debt introduces the process that makes slavery a matter of national interest. Since members of parliament as well as institutions are slave owners, English political culture is marked by the possession of slaves. This corrupts and enriches political parties on both sides. Beckles' evidence helps us understand why, faced with the idea that slavery was a national crime promoted by the abolitionists in the 19th century, English politicians argued that slavery was a matter of national interest. Another major contribution of this first part is the detailed presentation and analysis of the compensation received by British slave owners at the time of the 1838 abolition.

The second part, dedicated to action for reparations, traces the main events that have marked the last twenty-five years in this field with a description of the actions that preceded the Durban conference in 2001, but also developments in the struggle for reparations after that conference. It consists of four chapters examining, respectively, the principles of legal action for reparations, the behavior of the United Nations on the issue of reparations at the Durban conference, the British policy of "no apology, no reparations" and finally the reparation movement in the Caribbean.

Hilary Beckles' argument in Britain's Black Debt is supported by a bibliography rich in quantity and quality (22 pages of references) of books, articles, documentary films, reports and other archives. The author's argument is supported by extensive references in the form of notes grouped by chapters at the end of the book, which refer to some of the most serious work. Access to the references is further facilitated by the presence of a thematic index and authors' names. A number of tables provide additional readability, such as the one concerning mortality on Caribbean plantations, or the one presenting the figures for compensation received by slave owners.

Britain's Black Debt describes the fierce Anglo-American opposition (214) to the reparation movement before, during and after Durban conference.

Beckles reports European reprisals against heads of state who make demands for reparations, or who advance the movement (216 - 217). Hilary Beckles also sets out the arguments that motivate a legal action for reparations that should be taken against the British state and a number of its national institutions such as chambers of commerce, banks, insurance companies, and the Church of England.

Britain's Black Debt defines the character of this claim for reparation to be a government-to-government legal action in the first instance. It would also be addressed to the social and financial institutions that participated in the slave system and that still exist today (163). Beckles lists the other European states involved, Spain, Portugal, France, the Netherlands, Germany, Russia, Sweden, Norway and Denmark, outlining their involvement. The accusation is based on the fact that these countries benefited from the sale and enslavement of Africans. States should be held primarily accountable for their actions as institutions that passed and enforced laws allowing the enslavement of Africans. Secondly, they should be accountable for their implementation of fiscal incentives (165).

Another major thrust of this book is the presentation of the action of pan-African and Caribbean organizations during the decade 2000, which led the movement to move to the stage of legal action against the beneficiaries of the African slave trade and slavery, after the decision was taken to establish a commission to study legal actions to obtain reparation for African descendants. Beckles highlights the role played by the Barbados National Commission on Law and Order, which is the first to call on the Barbadian government to include the issue of reparation among the actions to be taken at the international level.

Hilary Beckles' approach in this book is both professional and personal. Beckles draws on the past and recent work of scholars from a variety of disciplinary fields. The work of jurists, philosophers, and economic historians are secondary sources of quality that are solicited to support her discourse. Among the many references, it is worth mentioning the place given to the work of historian Erick Williams or the more recent work of Barbara Solow, an economist at Harvard University, whose book is entitled British Capitalism and Caribbean Slavery: The Legacy of Eric Williams (1987). The use of the work of Boris Bittker, Richard Dunn, David Eltis, Joseph Inikori should also be noted. In addition, it is particularly important to note that Hilary Beckles situates her work in the legacy of the work of the Caribbean scholars CLR James, Walter Rodney Eric Williams. Gordon Lewis, among others, who through their work strived over the decolonization of consciences and demonstrated the existence of a Caribbean culture as viable as it is singular, restoring the humanity of former colonial subjects.

Hilary Beckles' speech is also based on primary sources collected over a long period of time by this researcher in social history, one of the leading specialists on slavery in the Atlantic world. Other primary sources, such as the statements made in the British Parliament during the debate on the bicentenary of the abolition of the slave trade by Great Britain, are also included in the text of this book, which invites the reader to go back and forth between the contemporary period and that of Modern Times or the nineteenth century. This characteristic helps to reinforce a major idea developed in this work, that of the continuity of the dynamics and effects of the slave trade and the enslavement of Africans in the British Caribbean colonies.

This book also builds on the fieldwork of Hilary Beckles, an actor in the reparation movement in the Caribbean and elsewhere, having represented Caribbean organizations and institutions at several important conferences on the issue of reparations. Hilary Beckles also chaired the Scientific Committee of the Slave Route Project set up by UNESCO in 1994.

Britain's Black Debt was written following the United Nations World Conference against Racism, Discrimination, Xenophobia and Intolerance held in Durban, South Africa, in 2001, to denounce the final resolution that European countries that implemented and benefited from African slavery in the Caribbean and the Americas succeeded in having adopted at the cost of blatant political positioning, the neo-colonial character of which Beckles denounces. Beckles outlines the issues addressed by this resolution, which states that slavery and the slave trade were not crimes against humanity at the time they were implemented, but "should have been". Hilary Beckles undertakes a rebuttal of this position and argues that its adoption was intended to prevent the establishment of a legal basis for a reparation process and the payment of compensation to victims or their heirs.

Britain's Black Debt turns out to be a book presenting and developing the "post-Durban" reparations discourse developed by transnational civil society organizations calling on Caribbean governments to take concrete actions to advance reparation action. It is the result of a request from Hilary Beckles by these various organizations in the Caribbean, Africa, North America, and Europe who asked him to write the text of an argument that would enable Caribbean people to take concrete action to obtain reparations. For this reason, this book is a text that brings together the elements needed to access a global vision of the history of the Atlantic world, which provides the basis for an argument that would enable legal action to be taken before international jurisdictions competent in international law.

The circumstances of its elaboration give it a contradictory stylistic tone that reflects a political intention perfectly assumed by the author. Beckles explains the tensions and power relations surrounding the Caribbean and African reparations movement by the fact that the British and some

Western nations reject the paradigm shift towards which the Caribbean and pan-African reparations movement is leading. He cites Lord Gifford's commentary on the Abuja conference in preparation for Durban:

> What deeply disturbs the British in the concept of reparations is that it completely changes the basis of the dialogue between blacks and whites, North and South, Europeans and Africans. Instead of requests for help from African countries delivered by a kind and charitable Europe, the Abuja Conference sought justice from a Europe that had committed crimes (179).

Britain's Black Debt not only collects historical facts, but calls for changes in perspectives and paradigms. It constitutes a counter-archive, as its sweeping of the history of the Atlantic world since modern times builds a new way of thinking. *Britain's Black Debt* becomes a new archive, a generating system governing production and the emergence of assertions that allow Caribbean people to envision the future with new ideas about history. It compels its reader to apprehend History and to conceive the future through new conceptions, for a liquidation of the negative legacy of colonization on all shores of the Atlantic Ocean and for a social transformation that repairs all the protagonists of the history of this region since Modern Times. This is expressed in the preamble of this important book:

The reparation of which I speak constitutes the final liberation, the universal recognition of truth, two necessary conditions for cultural and racial redemption in the postmodern evolution of man towards dignity and morality. The demand for reparation is a call for collective healing to close this chapter of history together (xvi).

REPARATIONS —An an urgent requirement for humanity

Slavery, Reparation, where's the anachronism ?

By Rosa Amelia Plumelle-Uribe

Colombian, author of several books on the slave trade, slavery and colonial domination.

In this contribution, we analyze the deportation of Africans to the concentration camps in America, their enslavement, the legal reparations related to this crime and the arguments put forward by opponents of the principle of reparations. For methodological reasons, we have chosen the most frequently used hostile arguments, those that are put forward on the radio, television, newspapers or even in conversations when Reparations are discussed. Some of them are listed below:

The arguments put forward by opponents of the Reparation Principle

Argument number one: When Europeans first arrived in Africa, the slave trade had long existed because slavery was an ancient practice on the continent.

Argument two: If Black People really want reparations, they will have to go to the Arab-Muslims first, because they were the first ones who started the African slave trade.

Third argument: European traders mostly bought slaves that the same Africans sold locally, acting as intermediaries between African slave traders and European planters in

America.

Fourth argument: At the time of the events, these atrocities were not a crime, so we cannot interpret and judge facts from two centuries ago with today's criteria, therefore, demanding reparation for these facts is a lamentable anachronism.

Analysis of the arguments

The argument explaining that transatlantic slave trade is said to have been a long-standing practice in Africa is a common insult used by negrophobes in the 19th century in the following terms: "*...We are asking, what crime have committed men who went to Africa to take the black people from Africa and transplant it here, thus substituting the civilized and Christian master from the barbarian master (...)? Those whom a benevolent destiny designated for this exodus left, not a homeland, but a bloody mass grave (...). What! You are reproaching us for this slavery that we did not create for you, since you were already slaves, while we took you away from human sacrifices...*"[1].

This manifestation of hatred raised as an argument by the heirs of the former European slaveholders, Christians and Jews, forged and conveyed the image of Africans who have a history of slavery practice and had the unfortunate habit of

---

[1] Newspaper *La Défense Coloniale* February 1882, released at Saint Pierre in Martinique and quoted by Victor Schoelcher in Colonial controversy, 1st volume, 1st issue 1882, 2nd issue, Fort de France, 1979, p.9

selling each other. This image still serves today to reinforce the feeling of moral superiority of the Europeans, whose corollary would be the inferiority of the Africans[2].

For this distortion of reality to become a commonplace, reality had to be ignored. That is to say that Europeans, far from having put an end to the slave trade after antiquity, continued to sell each other. So much so that in the 8th century, when Muslim, Arab and Berber Islamic slave traders arrived in Europe and colonised part of Spanish territory, the European slave trade, which had hitherto been intra-European, became international[3].

European Christians sold other Europeans, often Christians as well, to Jewish merchants trading between certain European countries and the Muslim world. In other words, there is no moral superiority of Europeans over Africans. For not only did Europeans sell other Europeans, they even set up castration centres in Europe, notably in Verdun, run by Jewish merchants, to make eunuchs in great demand by Muslim buyers[4].

The second argument is that if Blacks want reparation,

---

[2] Just take a look at the list of lies and dithering spat in the magazine L'HISTOIRE N° 878/February 2020 in line with the speech issued in the newspaper *La Défense coloniale*.

[3] For an exhaustive study on the subject, see *L'esclavage dans l'Europe Médiévale 'Slavery during tht time of Medieval Europe)* by Charles Verlinden, tome 1, Belgium, 1957 and tome 2, Belgium, 1977.

[4] See in *l'Espagne musulmane au Xe siècle*, (Muslim Spain in the 10th Century) by Evariste Lévi-provençal, Paris, Maisonneuve Larose, 2002

they must first turn to the Arab-Muslims, because they are the ones who inaugurated the trade in human beings in Africa. Certainly, in the middle of the 15th century,

When the Portuguese landed in Africa, Muslim slavers had, for seven or eight centuries, already transformed certain regions of the continent into a reservoir of slaves shipped to Muslim countries[5]. But that is not the point. The question is this: "*Why should the descendants of Africans deported to America be addressed to Arab-Muslims?*" They have nothing to do with them.

The slave traders who forced millions of African men, women and children to cross the Atlantic, shackled in chains in slave ships at the bottom of the hold, were not Arab-Muslims. And in the concentration camp world of America, the slavers who made them work until they died were not Arabo-Muslims either, they were Europeans, some of them Christians, some of them Jews[6]. Therefore, not only is it inadmissible, it is also indecent to say that the Blacks, descendants of Africans deported to the concentration camp in America, should demand reparations first from the

---

[5] Read Murray Gordon's *L'esclavage dans le monde musulman VII-XX siècle*, Robert Laffont, 1987 and also *Les négriers en terre d'islam (the slave traders in the land of Islam)* by Jacques Heers. *La première traite des Noirs VII-XXe siècle (the first slave trade VII-XXth century)*, Perrin 2004

[6] About slave traders role and jewish slave traders all along the slavery trade, read Jose Gonçalvez Salvador's os Magnatas do trafico negreiro séculos XVI e XVII, Universidade de Sao Paolo, Brasil and Plumelle-Uribe's, *Victimes des esclavagistes musulmans chrétiens et juifs (Victims of Jewish, Muslim and Christian slave traders)*, Anibwe 2012.

Muslims on the grounds that they were the first slave traders.

The third argument is related to the first. It serves to reinforce the prejudice that the trade in human beings was an exclusively African-African affair. This is why the discourse of Christian and Jewish slave traders, taken up by specialists working on this subject, is conveyed and amplified by all means. This historical narrative is very important because it instrumentalizes the local complicities enjoyed by European slave traders in Africa and at the same time conceals the African resistance drowned in blood.

The first attacks significantly devastating for Africa were made by the Portuguese who, in the middle of the 15th century, were in the vanguard of navigation. The resistance of the Africans, who were not familiar with firearms, was crushed in blood by the artillery of the Portuguese who used them with a bloody violence hitherto unknown in these countries. We know that there were *many resistances such as the one in Mombassa attacked in 1505:*

"With the help of African allies, the inhabitants fight the Portuguese in the streets of the city, all the way to the king's palace. Having stormed the palace, the Portuguese forced the king to surrender. The city was ransacked and burned to the ground. In 1528, Mombassa was attacked again. After four months of occupation, the Portuguese razed the city to the ground. But forty years later, in 1569, Mombassa was repopulated. Around 1586, the city was again razed to the ground and the king's head was taken and exhibited in Goa, India, where the representative of the king of Portugal in the

Indian Ocean[7] had his main residence."

Whatever local complicity the slave traders may have enjoyed, the fact remains that, in the concentration camp world of America, the enslavement of Africans and their descendants was the strict responsibility of Western slavers, both Christian and Jewish, as well as of the States that even legally regulated these crimes against humanity.

The fourth argument, like the previous ones, is a common place where the opponents of Reparations, whether ignorant, intellectuals or specialists, come together to explain to us in the most condescending way, that anachronisms should be avoided. They claim that the demand for Reparations legally related to the crimes of the slave trade and slavery would be an anachronism that consists in judging and interpreting facts that are centuries old, with today's principles and values. And they argue that at the time of the events these atrocities did not violate any legal norms and were not even perceived as a crime.

According to a widespread opinion, before the Enlightenment it was unthinkable even to condemn the couple of slave-treaters as we do today. For such condemnations would have become possible thanks and only thanks to the thinking of the 18th century philosophers, of which the French Revolution and the Declaration of

---

[7] From Louise Marie Diop-Maes, *Afrique Noire Demographie, Sol et histoire (Demography, Land and history)*, Présence Africaine, pp. 206-207, from *l'Histoire générale de l'Afrique (General history of Africa)*, volume 5, chapitre 25 ;

Human Rights were the extension.

During the 13th century, five centuries before the Enlightenment, the French Revolution and the Declaration of Human Rights, the Manden Charter, proclaimed in 1222 in the first capital of the empire of Mali, did indeed declare in its article 1 that "All [human] life is a life" and that "a life is no more respectable than any other life. Just as one life is not superior to another life"; in article 2 of the Declaration, it is stated that "Since every life is a life, any harm done to a life requires reparation ..."; and in articles 5 and 6 slavery is banished from the Manden[8]. And in order to keep this declaration out of the realm of rhetoric, the Manden authorities waged a war to the death against the Muslim slavers there.

And if less than a century and a half later, the scourge of slavery and the trade in human beings, like a cancer, was growing again everywhere in Mali under the reign of the Muslim emperors, this lamentable regression would not be able to change one iota the reality of the anti-slavery principles that guided the fight of the abolitionists of the Mande at the beginning of the 13th century.

In the 17th century, four centuries after the Manden Charter, shortly before the publication in France of the decree of

---

[8] Youssouf Tata Cissé, *la Charte du Manden, Du Serment des chasseurs à l'abolition de l'esclavage*, (the Manden Charter , an excerpt from the hunters oath to the abolition of slave trade) Lisbonne, Triangle Dankoun 2015

1685, known as the Black Code, and several decades before the Enlightenment, an event took place that specialists in the slave trade and slavery chose to say nothing about: Two Capuchins, the Spaniard Francisco José de Jaca and the Frenchman Épiphane de Moirans, in addition to the Scriptures and theology, sought the light of reason and human rights.

Arriving in the concentration camp in America, the Capuchin priest Francisco José de Jaca, sent by his Congregation to preach the Gospel, was terrified by the atrocities which he perceived as the absolute ugliness of evil in all its dimensions. Very soon he became openly hostile to this system which he called criminal. And very soon he also became the target of prosecution by civil and ecclesiastical authorities. Arrested and imprisoned, de Jaca was finally expelled and sent back to Spain via Cuba.

In Havana, de Jaca met the French missionary Epiphane de Moirans who had also been sent to spread the word of the Gospel in the New World. In Cayenne, where he exercised his ministry, the daily horror intrinsic to this concentration camp universe violently offended the human sensitivity of this Capuchin. And very quickly he began to preach the abolition of slavery as well as the payment of REPAIR to the victims and/or their heirs. This was much more than the French civil authorities and his ecclesiastical hierarchy could tolerate. The Priest of Moirans was therefore prosecuted, arrested and finally dismissed as well.

Following their meeting, these two missionaries united their will, strength and capacity to work for the abolition of slavery and the payment of REPAIR to the victims. Back in Europe, unlike Monsieur Montesquieu in the following century, de Jaca and de Moirans were not content with parlor ironies about slavery and slaves. They fought a long battle at the royal court in Spain and the papal court in Rome. Thanks to the support of some personalities, presumably in favour of their fight against the crime of slavery, they managed to bring their denunciations and petition to the king. It is noteworthy that in a Memorandum addressed in 1681 to the King of Spain, Charles II, the Priest of Jaca entitled "Human Rights" ("humanos derechos") the first part of his Memorandum.

In his Memoir entitled "*Free slaves or the legal defence of the freedom of slaves*", de Moirans uses the word deportation whenever he refers to the slave trade. And in the chapter entitled "*The masters of the Blacks are obliged to return the fruits of their labour*", de Moirans states bluntly: "*the masters are not only obliged to restore to the Blacks their freedom, but also to give them compensation for all the harm they have had to endure because of this alienation*".

These abolitionists literally harassed the Congregation for the Propagation of the Faith, on which they depended as missionaries, so that it would submit to the Holy Office of the Inquisition a questionnaire containing the essence of their demands for the abolition of slavery and REPAIR to the victims. The official result of this long struggle is a document dated March 20, 1686, in Rome. Here are some answers to the questions asked:

Thursday 20 March 1686

Decree of the Holy Office on several doubts submitted to it by the Sacred Congregation for the Propagation of the Faith.

Is it lawful to capture with violence or deception blacks and other non-belligerent savages? Their eminences say it is not lawful.

Is it lawful to buy or sell blacks and other non-belligerent savages captured with violence or deception and to bargain about them in any other way? Their eminences say it is not lawful.

Should the masters of blacks and other non-belligerent savages captured with violence or deception set them free? Their eminences say they must.

Are purchasers of Blacks and other non-belligerent savages, captured with violence or deception, and the masters, obliged to compensate them for the damages suffered? Their eminences say they are obliged [9] to do so.

---

[9] By Louis Sala-Molins, ESCLAVAGE, REPARATION, les Lumières des capucins et les lueurs des Pharisiens (the Lights of capuchins and glows of Pharisees, Paris

Conclusion

Francisco José de Jaca and Epiphane de Moirans paid a high price for this fight for the abolition of slavery and the REPAIR to the victims of this crime against los humanos derechos. And this even before Mr. Colbert had the initiative to create the legal monstruosity that we know as the "black code", designed to regulate "the most chilling genocide of modernity[10]".

In 1689, de Moirans (45 years old) died in France in the convent of Tours and Jaca (44 years old) died in Spain near Madrid. These abolitionists sacrificed everything in the fight for the freedom of Blacks and for reparations to be paid to the victims of this crime and to the beneficiaries. If their names remain unknown and absent from the history textbooks on the slave trade and slavery, it is because what we call historical knowledge has always been nothing more than the narrative or account of the interpretation made by those who have enough power to impose their vision.

These Capuchins not only considered trafficking and slavery to be a crime against human rights, they demanded an immediate end to this crime and the payment of reparations to the victims. They took this demand to the Royal Court of Spain and even to the Vatican. They did not wait until the

---

[10] By Louis Sala-Molins, le code noir ou le calvaire de Canaan (the Black Code and the Canaan ordeal)

Enlightenment to condemn in fact and in law the enslavement of Blacks in the American concentration camp. If, as we have pointed out, Article 2 of the Manden Declaration states that "Any harm done to a life requires reparation", and if in the 17th century the two Capuchins mentioned fought for the abolition of the slave-treaty couple and for reparations to be paid to the victims of this crime, as well as to their heirs,

Where then does the anachronism lie ?

The Curse of Cham, a vast sham

By René Louis Parfait Etile

Martinican Egyptologist

It seems difficult for Negroes to talk about their own suffering. These two examples should be enough: Not a single monument to the memory of the more than 20 million massacred Negroes has been built in the former Belgian Congo. Yet the President of the country is going to pray on the "Wailing Wall"! How long did it take Senegal to remember the Thiaroye massacre committed by France? We must therefore greet with respect and gratitude the sisters and brothers of MIR.

ACT 1: Put an end to the biblical obsession

For the West and for almost all the countries formerly colonized by "leukodermis" people, the "Holy Land" corresponds geographically to Israel, including the annexed Syrian territory from the Golan Heights (around the region of Baniyas, Paneas or Caesarea Philippi) and the territories under Palestinian authority (West Bank and Gaza Strip) to the southern coast of Lebanon (with Tyr and Sidon) and part of Jordan (Bethany beyond the Jordan River). This land also plays a role in the birth of Islam, since Islamic tradition places there Muhammad's celestial journey from the future esplanade of Al-Aqsa in Jerusalem.

However, here is what science says from the very mouth of

Israeli researchers : "...*The central historical core of the Pentateuch and Deuteronomistic history was composed, in broad outline, during the seventh century BC. The historical saga told in the Bible ... owes nothing to any miraculous revelation; it is brilliantly produced by human imagination ... the Israel Exodus saga taken out of Egypt is not historically true ...*" (The Bible Revealed, by Israel Finkelstein and Neil Asher Silberman).

Even more: "*Although a great deal of the biblical account takes place in Ancient Egypt, Abraham, Joseph, Moses are not to be found in the present state of archaeological research. (...) There is no archaeological evidence of their existence (existence of the Hebrew people) as described in Genesis and Exodus. (...) Is it possible that a population that lived in the land of Egypt for 430 years, 210 of which were spent in slavery under several pharaohs, could have fled this land and defeated the entire Egyptian army? Is it possible to settle in the land of Canaan without any reaction from the Pharaonic authority, knowing that throughout its history Egypt has been administering this province. (...) Why have 200 years of research in the sand, in tombs and in temples proved nothing?*" (The Secrets of Exodus, Messod and Roger Sabbah).

It is a scientifically proven fact that Semitic scriptures are posterior to the Pharaonic hieroglyphics. The oldest text found in Arabic dates only from 328 AD; it is from the tomb of an Arab chieftain in Nemra, near Damascus. Now the Arabs believe that only the Koran allows to know God! Hebrew is in fact a well-known Canaanite dialect. According to the Hebrew tradition itself, the Hebrew people adopted the language and places of worship of Canaanites. However, after glosses of El Armana (Upper Egypt) [letters written in the Babylonian language and in cuneiform characters by the small Palestinian vassals of the 15th century B.C. to the Pharaoh of Kemet Amenophis IV (Akhenaten)], the oldest monument in the Canaanite language is the triumphal inscription of the Moabite king Mesha (about 900 B.C.).

Yet, the Jews keep teaching that Saints understand only Hebrew and that God Yahweh would speak only Hebrew, while understanding other languages!

From the Reuters news agency report of December 15, 1998 (9:45 a.m.), the director of the German Archaeological Institute, Günter Dreyer, said: *"We thought Sumerians were the pioneers of writing. She pointed out to the international scientific community that a German team of archaeologists had made important discoveries in Africa. This new information force international researchers to simply proclaim the autopsy of the thesis of the invention of writing in Mesopotamia. Indeed, in Abydos (400 km south of Cairo), Professor Dreyer's team found about 300 potteries in an ancient royal cemetery. The hieroglyphic inscriptions discovered on them date from 3,400 BC, well before the appearance of cuneiform writing. So, Africa, the "Cradle of Humanity", is also the true "Cradle of Writing"*.

Even the Bible situates a good part of the famous "Garden of Eden" in Africa since: A river came out of Eden to water the garden. From there, it divided into four arms. The name of the first: Pichôn. According to the Hebrew, the word "Pichôn" means "the Nile". The second river mentioned in the Bible is called Guihon, in the Land of Kush, south of Kemet. Therefore, it is also called the Nile.

Writings of ancient Greeks prove the spiritual anteriority among the Negroes. For example, let us quote: "*Yesterday Zeus went to the side of the Ocean to take part in a banquet among the Negroes without reproach, and all the gods followed him. In twelve days from now, he will go back to Olympus.* " (Iliad I, 423-425, Homer); Ulysses weeping on Triptolomew says: "*I have seen nothing more beautiful than the divine Memnon.*" (Allusion to Memnon, king of the Negroes; see Odyssey XI, 522, Homer).

Concerning primitive Christianity, let us add some obliterated facts: Earthly existence or not, the oldest representations of Jesus, Jesus Christ and also of his mother Mary are black skinned. (See for example the oldest Last Supper in Roman Catacombs and the oldest representation of Mary and the Child; for Jesus Christ see the Coptic papyrus). Let us note that the oldest Marian "apparition" is located in Le Puy-en-Velay (Black Virgin). It is acknowledged that "Black Virgins" are in fact avatars of the "goddess Isis" (in fact she is a divine manifestation and her real African name is Aséta who will give Aïssatou).

"Texts of the Pyramids", Kamits (understand Negroes) texts of Pharaonic Egypt (Kémèt) engraved from Pharaoh Ounas (Vth dynasty), present the oldest religious writings, the oldest sacred writings, the oldest spiritual writings in the History of Humanity, until proven otherwise!

Why should the "black race" have been cursed, when the Black Continent saw the birth of not only the first Homo sapiens but also of the oldest writings addressed to the Divinity? A vast hoax of greedy racists and criminals?

ACT 2 : The well-known curse and some of its avatars

Noah's drunkenness is a biblical episode reported in Genesis 9:18-29. It includes the curse of Canaan, son of Ham (Ham, Kam), himself the son of Noah. The racist prejudice of color attached to the curse of Ham will be born late in the exegesis of a Father of the Church, Origen (182-254).

In order to give legitimacy to slave raids and the black people slavery, Whites used this old story, until then, seldom used in the Western world, the one about the curse of Cham. Pope Nicholas V and the Catholic Church blessed this crime against humanity on January 8, 1454; the black man became a "personal property" (Article 44 of the Black Code). Hence, Professor Louis Sala-Molins rightly says: "*The Law of Moses, Canaanites, Africans? The slavery of Canaanites was a pretext for the slavery of Africans? Yes, it all does make sense...*" (The Black Code or the Canaan Ordeal).

Biblical comments of rabbis that have led to racism and hatred of Negroes are khazars. They have almost nothing to do with the historical Hebrews (see for example Shlomo Sand (How has the Jewish people story been made up). Some say that Ham emasculated Noah in the darkest part of the night: for this reason the children of Canaan will be born ugly and black. Their hair will become frizzy, because Ham would have twisted himself to see the nakedness of his father. Their lips will swell, for Ham mocked his father. Their sex will lengthen ignominiously, for Cham was disrespectful to his father's nakedness. Canaan would command his descendants to love theft and fornication, to hate their masters and to always lie (Babylonian Talmud Sanhedrin 72a-b, 108 b and Pesahim 113b; Tanhuma Buber Genesis 49-50; Tanhuma Noah 13,15; Genesis Rabbah 341). Others say that it was Canaan that emasculated Noah (Tanhuma Buber Genesis 48-49; Genesis Rabba 338-40; Pirqe Rabbi Eliezer, ch. 23). A passage from the Midrash adds sodomy to the "crimes" of Ham.

The greatest rabbinic authority of recent centuries, Rabbi Moses Maimonide (1138-1204) also described "origins of Satan" (sic). It is about a fallen angel named "Black Sammael", who is said to have come to seduce Eve in the Garden of Eden (in the absence of Adam). From his union with Eve would have been born Cain. He would also have fornicated with Adam. This same Rabbi (Maimonide) in a work considered by the Jews to be the greatest in Jewish religious philosophy (The Guide of the Wanderers, Book III, Chapter 51) tells us of the Black People: "...*their nature is similar to that of dumb animals, and in my opinion they do not attain the rank of human beings; among existing things they are inferior to man, but superior to the ape, for they possess to a greater extent than the ape the image and likeness of man*".

Muslims are not "innocent". For example, Al-Idrisi, an Arab geographer born in 1100 (the most widely read geographer in the West at the time) believed that blacks were by the force inferior by nature, and he naturally supported the idea that their unfortunate destiny, especially to live as slaves, was due to the fact that they were born in the worst of all climates.

Al-Dimeshkri, around 1300, a good Muslim and author of a Cosmography, wrote about Blacks: "*No divine law has been revealed to them. No prophet has shown himself to them... Their mentality is close to that of animals...*"

We can read under the pen of the Arab historian Ibn Khaldun (1332-1406): "*It is true that most negroes easily become accustomed to servitude; but this disposition results, as we have said elsewhere, from an organizational inferiority that brings them closer to raw animals. Other men may have consented to enter a state of servitude, but it was with the hope of attaining honor, wealth and power*" (The Prolegomena, IV). Let us add: "*...malodorous disproportionate limbs, defective spirit and depraved passions ...*"

ACT 3: The African historical anteriority and the spirituality of Kémèt atomize the anti-nigger curses.

Let us begin with a criticism of the Torah (which corresponds to some texts close to the Old Testament of the Bible). There is no original belief in eternal life or in the resurrection of the righteous in Israel. Souls of the dead, both righteous and wicked, were sinking into Sheol, the kingdom of the dead and a ghostly place filled with wandering shadows. It is enough to read in Ecclesiastes 9:2: "*It is the same for all of us: a single fate for the righteous and the wicked, for the good and the bad, for the pure and the impure, for the one who sacrifices and the one who does not sacrifice*". *In fact, from the very beginning of creation, the famous god Yahweh forbade eternal life for humans: "The Lord God said, 'Behold, man has become like one of us, for the knowledge of good and evil. Let us now prevent him from putting forth his hand, from taking from the tree of life, from eating from it, and from living forever.* " Genesis 3:22. Only in the second century B.C. did the notion of the soul appear! (See Book of Daniel and second Book of Maccabees).

The African origin of Homo sapiens being an acquired fact, all religious people who do believe in a "Curse of Cham" should admit that their God is a "King of fools". In the Thora, the Bible and the Kuran, it is commonly admitted that Humanity was created in the image of God. It has already been scientifically proven that Negroes were the first ones to be on earth, whether the "White Supremacy" like it or not ! The sole fact concurr to destroy any racist assumptions.

Here is a (non-exhaustive) list of Negro concepts which are all scientifically attested facts by hieroglyphic writings. Sources are numerous and all are anterior to the writing of the Torah, the Bible and the Koran. We will simply cite only one source for each of the concepts.

Concept of the oneness of the Divinity (The Great Hymn to Aten); concept of "Holy Land", "Divine Land": it is the "To Nétèr", Land of the Divinity located at the level of the African

Great Lakes south of Kémèt (T. Bardinet, Les Papyrus médicaux de l'Égypte pharaonique); Concept of "Divine Light" : it is Raou Ra (Texts of the Sarcophagi); Concept of Prayer: the oldest written prayers (Texts of the Pyramids); Concept of Soul and Angel (Texts of the Pyramids); Concept of the weighing of the Soul (Papyrus of Hounefer); Concept of Resurrection (the oldest attested written resurrection is that of Osiris, see for example Papyrus of Ani); Concept of Eternal Life (Texts of the Pyramids); Concept of the Trinity (Temple of Luxor : Amun-Ra/Mout/Khonsu); Concept of the "Immaculate Conception" (conception of Horus son of Isis and Osiris, funerary Temple of Pharaoh Sethi I); Concept of the Sharing of Bread, Wine (Texts of the Sarcophagi); Concept of Communion (A. Moret, Kings and Gods of Egypt); Concept of the Sacred Heart: the so-called Latin cross on the heart is an attribute of Osiris (Hieroglyph Nefer which means "good, perfect, beautiful"); Concept of the Cross (the cross Ankh is a sign of eternal life); Concept of Holy Water (Texts of purification rituals ; Sacred lakes of Kemet, especially the Sacred Lake of the Temple of Karnak); Concept of Incense (Bas-relief, offering of incense by Pharaoh Sethi I, Temple of Osiris in Abydos); Concept of Baptism (that of Pharaoh Amenhotep I by Anubis and Maat, Valley of the Kings); Concept of Heaven and Hell (Paradise: Fields of Ialou, Tomb of Sennedjem, Dayr al-Madina / Hell: the fire of the "burning wells" into which the damned will be thrown, Tomb of Sethi I, Valley of the Kings); Concept of Diabolic Serpent (Book of Gates, Tomb of Ramses I, Valley of the Kings); Concept of Divine Commandments: 42 Commandments also called "the Negative Confession" or "Commandments of the

MAAST" (Papyrus of Ani); Concept of Passion (The Passion of Osiris and his death by the Sethians, Texts of the Pyramids); Concept of disciples (Horus son of Osiris enthroned before his 12 disciples, Books of the Hereafter, seventh hour of Amdouat); Concept of Cross (Cross Ankh, Cross of Eternal Life, Texts of Pyramids); Concept of the Symbolism of the Fish (Symbol of Ousiré, because drowned in the Nile, then cut into 14 pieces, his phallus was swallowed by a fish / Osiris in the form of a fish, Tomb of Khabeknet, 19th dynasty); Concept of the Way of the Cross (Passion of Osiris / following his murder, the 14 pieces of his body, scattered over the territory of Kemet, are at the symbolic origin of the 14 steps of the Way of the Cross of Jesus); let us quickly quote other Negro concepts: Palm Sunday (linked to Isis), the Osirian Feast of Easter, the descent into hell on the second day following his earthly death (for Osiris) and his ascension to heaven.

Finally it is good to note that the review "The World of the Bible" (number 216 March/April/May 2016) acknowledges the anteriority of the Kamite Spirituality over Christianity and all other religions (in particular the anteriority of the history of Osiris and his resurrection over that of Jesus)! You cannot say that this biblical review is pro-Kemet or even less pro-Negro!

CONCLUSION

We see that it is better to keep quiet, and look like a fool, than to open one's big mouth and leave no doubt about it. However, one of the great evils of this world is that, most of the time, criminal fools are the ones who win. We must unite our efforts and remain vigilant in the face of human stupidity (racism, self-proclaimed divine election, xenophobia, murder of the righteous ones, colonialism, modern slavery, persecution of the weak, misogyny, etc.). No scientific, legal, moral, etc. concession, in short, no "Maâtic" concession (of the Maât, Truth-Justice among the Kamits) should be granted to crimes against Humanity. Appropriate reparations must be systematically implemented. Yes, the Negro has a soul. It is not only a Negro concept, but also one of the most beautiful creations of human reason!

Slavery Reparation

From the book "Slavery Reparations - The Glow of the Capuchins and the Glow of the Pharisees." released by Ed. Lignes, September 22, 2014 (ISBN 978-2-35526-132-9)

By Louis Sala-Molins

Professor of Political Philosophy, specialist in the practices of the Roman Inquisition and the codification of black slavery

We would like to thank the publisher "Lignes" for his kind permission to use large extracts from this book:

"The political question of reparations due for the crime of the slave trade is going to be intensely debated. In the beginning of 2015 year, Louis Sala-Molins, the publisher of the Code Noir (13 editions), takes sides by presenting the books of anger of two Capuchins of the late seventeenth century, who demanded not only the immediate cessation of this infamy, but already unconditional reparations. "

We are very grateful to the author, Mr. Louis Sala-Molins, for his generosity and availability, who wrote for us this note presenting the two Capuchin monks of the end of the seventeenth century, who demanded not only the immediate cessation of the infamy of slavery, but already unconditional reparations :

" A few years before Versailles covered itself with glory by

promulgating the BLACK CODE, which legalized slavery and gave slaves the glorious status of "movable property" that could be exchanged for money like a beast of burden or the carp in a pond, Epiphane de Moirans and Francisco José de Jaca, in a powerful argument, put an end to any possible connection between slavery and the law: Considered as illegal, trafficking and slavery must end without delay. They enumerate the consequences, in law, of this legal act. Among them, this one: for the heinous purchase and the dreadful crossing of the Atlantic, for the unpaid work, the appalling labour imposed, the beatings endured, the torture and suffering inflicted, the punishments endured, the crimes perpetrated, total reparation is due not only to each slave living at the time of the abolition of slavery, but also to the rightful owners of each slave who died before that day, without any limitation in the number of generations."

Chapter: Prologue

Even today, cultural, economic and social consequences of so many centuries-old slavery still weigh heavily on the shoulders and minds of most descendants of the black slaves of yesteryear. No one denies this evidence.

The French genius has found definitive words to settle forever the question of reparations owed to black slaves and their heirs for the crushing work and the infinite sorrows endured throughout the interminable duration of their ordeal.

History records at least three of them as being the law. And, in addition to this, a silent gesture which, by omission, did no less than deny it.

Second Republic, 1848: second and final abolition of slavery in sugar islands of the Great Nation. Without in any way invading people's way of thinking at that time, rather insensitive to the plight of black people at the ends of the world, a question of... detail got raised. Deprived of everything, what would become of the Blacks, once slaves and all of a sudden emancipated? People get worry about it, one argues, one discusses. Pretty smoothly. Doesn't the justice that takes away their shackles and give them access to citizenship owe them reparations? Should it not distribute them, in whole or in part, the land that they have been ploughing, sowing, valuing with their arms, watering with their tears, fertilizing with their blood? The great Tocqueville, then considered as the conscience of the nation, from then on and today an inescapable reference of its wise morality, closes the debate: "If negroes have the right to become free, it is indisputable that colonists have the right not to get collapsed because negroes have been set free." Békés will sleep peacefully, they will not lose a single acre of their plantations. Better than that, they'll be compensated for the loss of their negroes. Righteous Second Republic...

Vth Republic, 2001: Taubira Law qualifying trafficking and slavery as "crimes against humanity". They are therefore imprescriptible. The text of the law wanted by the deputy of Guyana contained an "article 4" worded as follows:

"A *committee of qualified personalities shall be set up to determine the harm suffered and examine the conditions for*

119

reparation due in respect of this crime. The expertise and assignments of this committee shall be determined by decree of the Council of State".

As the representatives of the people understood that this article was not a mere embellishment, it was rejected by the Law Commission and ended up as quickly as it had appeared, in the dustbin.

After the Tocquevillian burst of brilliance of the French genius, launched with hoopla, destroying the issue of reparations, the mute gesture of the legislator in the antechamber of the Assembly dissociated "*imprescriptibility*" and "*crime against humanity*" that the language of laws had hitherto announced with a single breath. The omission having been evoked and regretted by two or three elected members of the Assembly, the French genius thundered in the voice of the (Garde des Sceaux) Minister of Justice of the then Socialist government, giving the appropriate reply: "*The government cannot be situated in a perspective of compensation that would be practically impossible to implement. Two-three votes having insisted in the Senate on the legal necessity to "repair", the Secretary of State for Overseas echoed the strong words of his colleague, the Minister of Justice, in the Senate by asking no further talks about reparations because "compensation and reparation are very complex issues".*

Compensation ? Reparation? An Absurdity according to Tocqueville. Irrelevant for the Law Commission. *Very complex or practically impossible* for two ministers in a socialist government. Each with definitive words - or gesture - , Tocqueville more than a century and a half ago, and after that a Law Commission, a Minister of Justice and a Minister for Overseas France, less than fifteen years ago: that is more than enough to found and establish "historical tradition".

And since there is now truth and historical tradition, what is the point of wasting time revising the upstream part of history and tradition that is so righteously founded?

The slavery of Blacks established by the monarchy? Commemorating it, the Fifth Republic condemns it and refers to the Second Republic, which put an end to it. Period.

"*End point*" of a reading in the wrong direction? No. Period. For this question of reparations, which is for the most part preposterous, essential if justice is not an empty word, has been dealt with, times and times again since slave ships made the triangular crossing bringing junk from the lands of Christendom to pagan Africa, deporting Blacks from Africa to the Americas, bringing back from Americas to Europe the products of the labour of those Black People deported and reduced to slavery.

Treated and solved by its evacuation out of the debate, sometimes in two peremptory sentences, sometimes at the end of an endless plethora of ratiocinations and convoluted syllogisms. Negroes and planters, bishops and governors, politicians and ministers, theologians and philosophers, traditionalists and reformists, revolutionaries and royalists will disagree on how to keep - the word is from Montesquieu

- *black slaves* day after day, *to put an end to slavery at the end of this or that moratorium without endangering social peace* - this is Condorcet's approach and concern - or, on the contrary, to strengthen and better regulate its practice in order to maintain and develop production and trade. However, they all agree that, when they evoke it, the question of a wage due to the emancipated man for his slave labour is considered, when they do evoke it, to be absurd, crazy, senseless in the strongest sense of the word. They say that he is free, but we are not going to push the zeal to the point of filling his pockets by emptying those of the masters.... The sound word of the great Tocqueville, immediately established as an irrefutable dogma of faith or as a founding political principle, a matter of taste, was nothing more than the haughty affirmation of a tacit consensus that had been maintained for centuries. In harmonious and immemorial agreement with the law. Naturally.

The cause is therefore understood: no compensation or reparation, this is the norm imposed in all truthfulness by tradition. Is this true?

Yet there is no shortage of scatterbrained people who, long after the abolition of black slavery, are seeking to quarrel with the successors of the slaveholders of yesteryear - states, nations, companies, lineages - and claim to force today's courts and powerful people to reopen the closed chapter of reparations. They made their voices heard in 2001 at the international conference in Durban. They are conducting remarkable, and sometimes victorious, legal actions in the United States. Associated in the MIR

(International Movement for Reparations) or under other acronyms, they intend to judicially question the French State, and not exclusively. Madness, they say, tradition and truth being the ones we have seen. Madness, they hammered out by high-ranking historians and essayists.

These people, through a valiant series of syllogisms, love to denounce in the scatterbrained of whom I speak a lack of intellectual probity that goes hand in hand with their ignorance. You broach, say the wise men to the fools, the weaknesses of the greats of the thought of yesteryear at the time of rendering justice to blacks exploited to death in slavery; you seek to quarrel with them because of their silence, or because of some muted criticism, or because of the devious nature of some passing accommodations of commercial practices to the achievements of reason; and questioning them over the centuries, you argue against them using the principles, words, and values of today; words, values, and principles which, let it be noted, would not be what they are today if they had not been the first to lay the premises and gather the first fruits in their time, the glorious time of the Enlightenment. Why do you want, wise men insist, that the thinkers you are thinking of would have imagined for a single moment that they would have had to evoke reparations due to the slaves, this issue, unthinkable at the time, having been invented from scratch in our season and not at all relevant to moral or legal preoccupations of their time? At that rate, you poor fools, you are browbeating them for not having demanded that they benefit from Social Security, paid holidays and marriage for all, including LDCs and FGM. Take it easy, you

123

funny bastards, and go play somewhere else: anachronism in history is an ugly flaw, they preach.

Having crowed, wise men conclude by praying that these fools just stop their indecent din.

They are right, the scolders: as far as history is concerned, worse than a mortal sin, anachronism is a sacrilege. To be avoided, therefore, like the plague. But it is anachronistic to broach a commonly accepted and temporally dated thought of the day before yesterday and to claim, in order to do so, criteria for the day after tomorrow.

Here are two examples of pernicious effects produced by this sacrilege in the world, serene or agitated, of historians.

First one : to wonder in our days why did Aristotle speak as calmly as we know about the existence of "*slavery by nature*" is utterly ridiculous. It has been known from the cradle that slavery in all its forms was as natural in the world of Plato and Aristotle as the daily course of the sun in the Greek sky, and no one could argue with that. However, Aristotle specifically underlines, when speaking about *natural slavery*, so natural that the matter is settled in half a paragraph of "Politics", that "*some people claim that natural slavery does not exist*" and that, consequently, only happening wars and banditry are the source of it. Who are these "*some*", whose foresight should be greeted by posterity? The great philosopher does not say: without fearing anachronism, he nevertheless says that they do exist... in contradiction with an undisputed general opinion and a commonly accepted thought, both of which are temporally dated.

Second one. Bartolomé de Las Casas. Indians. The Valladolid controversy. Order of the King: a question as fundamental to the legitimacy of the American adventure of Castile as that of Humanity and the natural freedom of Indians is being debated. The time has come for Aristotelian dogmatics to decide: neither full and complete humanity nor natural freedom among Indians, Aristotelian Sepúlveda pleads. Against him, Las Casas brings over other references and wins: the Indian is a free man. What about the Negro? One sentence for him, from a... blatant anachronism, in the impressive corpus of the Andalusian bishop's fights in favor of Indians: "*Blacks? They are like Indians*". As curt and definitive as that: just like the Indians enslaved at home, the black man deported from elsewhere is a free man. Can you imagine making such nonsense at a time when it was simply unthinkable?

Let's face it. No matter how loud people clamour in every period, there are always some big, or small, or eminent, or lowly, who go around blowing their lungs out, shouting their truth at the top of their lungs against the prevailing opinion. The history of historians is parsimonious and hears it when it pleases them. It's timeless...

The time has come for us to hear from a couple of scummy losers. Two Capuchins who, as the 17th century draws to a close, were struggling to demonstrate, based on the law, what wise men of the early 21st century consider to be the whim of four simpletons.

But first of all, since the case was pending, what did prosecutors say in our courts? It is short, simple and irrevocable: since the slave trade and slavery were in accordance with the legality of the time and since these practices did not contravene moral values of the time, there is no reason to continue by projecting from a distance more than a century old scruples of today, which transform the old and innocent routine of navigation, trade and work of the day before yesterday into a crime. Certainly, voices were once raised against the excesses of slavery, even against the slave system? So be it. But we do not know about any of them to have added to the demand for "abolition" a demand for "reparation", which is totally unimaginable. No anachronism in court. Each period has its truth. So, no case.

The plaintiffs are ordered to pay costs. Out of the goodness of our hearts, we spare them a fine for "contempt of court", just hang up the dress in the cloakroom and go home.

Excerpt from the chapter: The last word...

A singular document, dated 20 March 1686 in Rome, contains the official conclusion of the long struggle of two Capuchins in the Americas, at the Spanish Court and, finally, at the Pontifical Court, to acknowledge :

- The natural liberty of black people enslaved ;

- The absolute illegality of the slave trade and the market of which they are sold;

- The obligation of the immediate and universal emancipation of all black slaves without exception;

- The obligation to pay them or their descendants and successors in full, without limitation of time or number of generations, the wages due for their work;

- The obligation to compensate them or their dependants for the suffering endured and the mortal risks incurred from the day of their deportation from Africa or their birth in slavery in the West Indies to the day of their liberation.

***

FROM THE SAME AUTHOR on the slave trade and slavery of Blacks

- The Code Noir or the Calvary of Canaan, Paris, PUF. 1st ed: 1987; 12th ed: 2012

- The Miseries of the Enlightenment. Sous la raison l'outrage, Paris, Robert Laffont, 1992, out of print. Re-edition corrected and enlarged, Paris, Homnisphères, 2008

- Africa to the Americas. Le Code Noir espagnol, Paris, PUF, 1992

- 1492. Le choc de deux mondes (in collaboration), Geneva, La différence, 1993

- The chain and the link. A Vision of the Slave Trade (in collaboration), Paris, UNESCO, 1998.

- Déraison, esclavage et droit (in collaboration), Paris, Unesco, 2002

REPARATIONS —An an urgent requirement for humanity

Reparations, Africa and Pan-Africanism

By Mame Hulo (Guillabert)

Writer, Director of Diasporas Noires Editions

Member of the Pan-African Federalist Movement
Ambassador for Africa of the MIR

Introduction

I first heard about the MIR in 2017, when the president of the MIR Martinique Garcin Malsa, founder of the movement, having noticed my strong pan-African commitment, my books and conferences, as well as the creation of the publishing house Diasporas Noires, wished me to be the guest of honour at the 17th Konvwa Pou Réparasyon in Martinique.

I was truly honoured by this invitation, and very touched by the fierce and constant commitment to this cause of President Patriarch Malsa, I do confess that I took a big slap in the face during this trip by discovering a terrible and underhanded oppression of the people of Martinique, and which was in fact only a continuation in various "softer" forms of slavery and the Black Code, after the "so-called" abolition of slavery[11]. It is moreover, the same colonialism

---

[11] Read the book "**Zaïre and Theophile – No pity for niggers**" by Imaniye Dalila Daniel, it explains how this so-called abolition process led the way to

and the same oppression that continues in different forms after the "so-called" independence in almost all African countries called "francophone".

Since this landmark meeting, despite my numerous militant activities on various subjects related to Pan-Africanism and social issues in Africa, I have been trying to bring my energy and strength of conviction to the edifice of the MIR. I organised the first Konvwa Pou Reparasyon in Africa with the MIR; with the help of my little sister from Martinique Myriam Malsa, about a hundred people came to Gorée in Senegal for about ten days. MIR Senegal was founded in May 2019, created by young committed pan-Africanists, then the 2nd Konvwa in Africa took place in August 2019 in Benin with its share of very strong emotions...

Thanks to these actions of the MIR, more and more Pan-Africanists on the Continent are discovering, supporting and adhering to demands for reparations made by our African brothers and sisters who are descendants of AFRĒS (Africans Reduced to Slavery, because the first of the reparations advocated by the ICNP International Committee of Black People, consists in no longer calling our Ancestors "*slaves*").

Being a publisher, I had the idea to coordinate and edit this collective book on reparations to mark the anniversary of the 20th Konvwa Pou Réparasyon in May 2020, to applaude

---

forced labour and the detention of freed niggers inside plantations under pain of being put to jail for wandering if they were to be found outside the farms.

20 years of struggle by the MIR and its tireless president!

I would like to thank all contributors who have generously accepted to participate in this militant adventure, as well as Myriam Malsa, a member of MIR Martinique, who has been of great help to me concerning the coordination of this book.

Crimes to be repaired

Wars of domination, raids, massacres, deportation, enslavement, torture and atrocities of all kinds, colonialism, neo-colonialism, economic plunder, epistemic racism, discrimination, apartheid, mass poisoning, genocide by substitution, epistemicide, negationism, revisionism, etc., with irreparable psychological consequences over several centuries and more than often, irreversible.

One of those consequences is the terrible alienation of most Africans conditioned from childhood by lies and the superiority complex of their oppressors, educated by their school of alienation, their "hostage school" (the name given to the colonial school at its beginnings in Africa, because it was intended for sons of chiefs and kings who were taken hostage by force by the colonists, and today these hostages are the African elite).

"The colonized also succeeds, through religion, in ignoring the colonizer. By fatalism, all initiative is taken away from the oppressor, the cause of evil, misery and destiny being left to God. The individual thus accepts the dissolution

decided by God, flattens himself before the colonist and before fate and, through a kind of inner rebalancing, reaches a serenity of stone." Frantz Fanon in *"The Damned of the Earth"*.

Today, Black People, everywhere in the world, in spite of undeniable resistance, is in a situation of excessive vulnerability where EVERYTHING NEEDS TO BE REPAIRED, TO BE RESTORED: its spirit, its soul, its DNA and its link with its Ancestors, its spirituality, its culture, its History, its methodology of reflection, its relationship with science, its relationship with Nature, its philosophy, its self-esteem, etc., are all in need of repair.

All the knowledge Black People had been acquiring over hundreds of thousands of years, in fact since the appearance of modern man (Homo sapiens sapiens) in Africa, and which made him the oldest guide of Humanity on the path of human evolution, has been stolen, hidden, ransacked, falsified, erased WILLFULLY from his memory, but even more seriously from the memory of all Humanity.

"The Negro is unaware that his Ancestors, who have adjusted to the material conditions of the Nile Valley, are the most ancient of all guides of Humanity on the road to civilization; that it was they who created Arts, religion (especially monotheism), literature, the first philosophical systems, writing, the exact sciences (physics, mathematics, mechanics, astronomy, calendar...), medicine, architecture, agriculture, etc. at a time when the rest of the Earth (Asia,

Europe: Greece, Rome...) was plunged into barbarism." Cheikh Anta Diop *Alert in the Tropics,* Présence Africaine 2006

So, criminals against humanity have not been content to hunt down the Black People, to enslave them, to humiliate them, to deny them as human beings... They also committed the crime of epistemicide.

"Thus imperialism, like the hunter of prehistory, first kills the being spiritually and culturally, before seeking to eliminate it physically. The negation of the history and intellectual achievements of Black African Peoples is the cultural, mental murder that has already preceded and prepared for genocide here and there in the world. "

"I believe that evil, which the occupier has done to us, has not yet been cured, that's the fundamental issue. Cultural alienation ends up being part of our substance, part of our soul, and when you think you've gotten rid of it, there is still more to get rid of.

The fight we're being put into is one of the most violent fights we've ever had. (...) They deny you as a moral being, they deny you as a cultural being, they don't see the evidence, they close their eyes, they rely on your alienation, on your complex, on conditioning and subordination reflexes and on so many such factors. And if we do not know how to

emancipate ourselves from such a situation by our own means, there is no salvation."
Cheikh Anta Diop, Civilisation ou Barbarie, Présence Africaine, Paris, 1981.

The Portuguese sociologist Boaventura de Sousa Santos very often uses the term EPISTEMICIDE in his work as early as 1994 in several of his articles or books: *"The new paradigm constitutes an alternative to each of these traits. In the first place, there is not just a single form of valid knowledge. There are many forms of knowledge, as well as the social practices that generate and sustain them. Modern science is based on a practice of professional and social technical division of labour and on the endless technological development of the productive forces of which capitalism is today the only example. (...) The genocide that so many times characterizes European expansion was also an epistemicide: strange people were eliminated because they also had strange forms of knowledge, and these strange forms of knowledge were eliminated because they were based on strange social practices and strange people. But epistemicide has been much more extensive than genocide because it has always claimed to subjugate, subordinate, marginalize or outlaw practices and social groups that could be seen a threat to capitalist expansion, or during a good part of our century to communist expansion (on this point as modern as capitalism), and also because this has happened both in the peripheral and extra-North American space of the world system and in the central European and North*

American space, against workers, indigenous people, Blacks, women and minorities in general (ethnic, religious, sexual).

The new paradigm considers epistemicide as one of the great crimes against humanity."

Their goal was to erase their motivations, the evidence, to minimize their responsibilities as much as possible, to falsify the memories, denying the Humanity of the Black People, declaring it cursed by God, designating it as active and co-responsible for its own misfortune.

They therefore falsified History before, during and after their crimes, in order to destroy and complicate any possibility of identifying these crimes, their motives, their responsibilities, the prejudices and the appropriate reparations, their goal was to create a SITUATION THAT WAS NEVER IRREPARABLE, PERFECT CRIMES THAT NEVER WERE IMPUNISHED !

They were on the verge of achieving these goals, but they never take any account of the extraordinary fighting spirit of Black people on the long run, despite their general state of vulnerability as people that were oppressed and dominated for centuries, is today in the process of recovering its historical and spiritual heritage thanks mainly to the great and courageous scholar Cheikh Anta Diop and his ever-increasing number of African historian disciples, these people are on the road to rebirth despite these long centuries of enslavement, atrocities, falsifications and lies in all fields.

This miracle of resilience is, undeniably due, in its largest part, to the Pan-Africanism movement, its numerous leaders on all continents, and all our known or anonymous Resistance Ancestors, throughout the world and through time.

I note that according to Sesh Coovi Rekhmiré, one of the greatest Kemitologists, a disciple of Sheikh Anta Diop, initiator of the Pan-African University of Knowledge, the concept of Pan-Africanism dates back from Ancient Egypt and the Pharaoh Naré Mari (Narmer) and was called "Sematawy", Kemet's reunification process.

"I can think of fewer other examples in history of such strength of character, courage and faith in people who, as victims of such utterly inhuman oppression, not only saved their culture in a foreign land, but flourished it." Jean Ziegler (1980: 79) in the Revue Ethiopiques http://ethiopiques.refer.sn/spip.php?article1789

What needs repairing ?

Many Africans on the Continent and in the Diaspora believe that the reparations demanded of Criminals against Humanity, of whatever nature, cannot repair the immensity and enormity of the damage suffered over the centuries. Moreover, that we cannot lower ourselves into asking them, begging for recognition or reparations for their crimes. Even more again, that it would be a betrayal to monetize the incommensurable suffering of our Ancestors... and so on....

Beyond the understandable arguments of one side or the other, beyond the powerlessness of a dominated people against the one who has dominated it again and again for centuries, this powerlessness in the face of their contempt should in no way prevent this strong and courageous demand for justice and reparation for human dignity, even if it means shouting in the desert, the aim being not to let them sleep soundly in their autistic courts, for this cry will sooner or later find an echo in their barricaded conscience. Moreover, their recognition of their crimes as crimes against humanity came late, under the blows of the demands of Black militants. Reparations will follow this same path inexorably, sooner or later, especially when the criminals against humanity have been "repaired" after the "so-called" abolition of slavery.

Even if Black People still are under domination, this demand for justice must make its way and come back over and over, as a leitmotiv, until it being honoured! If this demand continues to be despised by Westerners, there will come a time when African People will once again become sovereign, will create its own courts to judge criminals against humanity, to FINALLY settle these heinous crimes and restore Harmony for all Humanity...

This is an urgent demand that goes beyond the future of the Black People alone!

As Frantz Fanon says in *"Les damnés de la terre"*: *"the great confrontation cannot be postponed indefinitely"*.

Reparation, an ancestral African wisdom to restore Harmony

Since the dawn of time, the concept of justice in Black Africa has invariably been accompanied by the concept of reparation. These reparations must be arbitrated, pronounced, proposed to the victims, accepted by the criminals, in order to achieve a return to peace, harmony and why not reconciliation.

In the presentation of the book *"Power and Justice in the Tradition of Black Peoples - Philosophy and Practice"* ed. **Harmattan, by Fatou Kiné Camara**, Doctor of Law, teacher-researcher at the Faculty of Law of the University of Dakar, disciple of Professor Cheikh Anta Diop, we read the following:

"Should we be content to see justice as nothing more than a machine for distributing penalty and punishment? In the negro-African conception of justice, judging is not about condemning, it is about trying to restore a broken harmony. "

Then in page 48 of the book in the chapter *"Justice, Daughter of Good"*:

"Who can still deny the remarkable advance of Negro-African criminal law in terms of humanism and rationality? The law of Talion, so much cherished by some civilizations, is only valid in Black Africa as long as it allows the person responsible for something, to know what he or she is exposing himself or herself to in case he or she does not pay damages to the victim. In fact, we have cited examples, most of these penalties amounted to only one, monetary compensation or compensation in nature. As for physical punishment, which is provided for in the Black Criminal Law, it is stated only in a comminatory manner. They serve only to assess the amount of compensation due.

Reparation, an alternative penalty to all other forms of punishment

Giving the choice between financial compensation or compensation in kind (e.g. cattle) and having an eye punctured, the victim does not hesitate for long. He hesitates even less since he has been imbued since childhood with a moral which is omnipresent in tales, proverbs, songs, pictorial art, etc. and which condemns this type of behaviour by making it look ridiculous. Stigmatized as the act of a stupid and wicked being, revenge is simply tolerated and firmly discouraged. The teaching of the African sage is that revenge is sterile."

Also in this book "***Power and Justice in the Tradition of Black People***" (page 53, chapter "*Justice as a Daughter of the Good*") the concept of reparation can be summarized by this sentence by Olawale Elias, Nigerian, Associate of Law and Doctor of Philosophy:

"*African law is a law aimed at preserving social equilibrium and harmony in the community, whereas European law in general is, in a very marked way, a law of sanctions. (...) The idea at the heart of African law is one of compensation and not punishment*".

Another African jurist, the Ivorian T. Ehui drives home the point by noting this major difference between the foundations of Western and African jurisdictions (page 54, chapter "*Justice as the Daughter of the Good*"):

"*In traditional African societies, the major objective of the trial was conciliation between the guilty party and the victim. In this sense, the aim was above all to compensate the victim and to make the offender aware of the seriousness of his act. Reconciliation was therefore a three-fold process: reconciliation of the offender with himself, of the offender with the victim, of the offender with society...*".

Finally, let us note this remarkable conclusion :

"*If there is one value at the heart of black civilizations, it is Harmony, and all means are good to establish, preserve and restore it every time it is shaken... Judges are not there to punish, but to help establish the truth, which is a prerequisite for the reconciliation of adversaries and the reparation of the social disorders that the conflict has revealed.* "

I would like to thank **Fatou Kiné Camara**, my sister and friend, the Author of this book "*Power and Justice in the Tradition of Black Peoples - Philosophy and Practice*" ed. Harmattan, whom I thank for agreeing to be widely quoted in this text and for providing me with excerpts from her work.

Pan-Africanism, the ultimate tool of self-repair of the Black People!

"*All people of African descent, whether they live in North or South America, in the Caribbean and in any other part of the world, are Africans and belong to the African Nation.* " said Kwame Nkrumah, former president of Ghana and one of the fathers of pan-Africanism.

"*The destiny of all black people anywhere in the world is linked to Africa. As long as Africa is not respected, black people will not be respected,*" added Nana Akufo Addo, current president of Ghana.

"*There is an African personality that is common to all black men and women; this personality contains specific values of wisdom, intelligence and sensitivity. Black People are the most ancient peoples of the earth. They are dedicated to*

141

unity and to a common future of power and glory.

This pan-African ideology therefore rejects any idea of assimilation, of integration into the universe of the dominator. This ideology of refusal of any assimilation is a motivational force of extraordinary power. History records that the African nationalist movement has taken on an extraordinary scale as a result of pan-Africanism". (Jean Ziegler, 1980: 78).

The ultimate reparation brought about by Pan-Africanism is the UNITY of the Black Peoples, their fraternal, cultural and political solidarity, and if necessary and desired, the legitimate return to their continent of origin, their Mother Earth.

For this to happen, Africans of all countries must work towards Reunification, the creation of the Federal State of the United African States (States within and outside the African Continent).

On the other hand, from now on, the African countries of the Continent have the imperative duty to set up as soon as possible, a reception facility for the descendants of African deportees from all over the world, following the example of Ghana, to give them nationality without any conditions, and to grant them free land, logistical means and fraternal assistance to settle at their request, and wherever they wish.

AFRICA'S CALL FOR ITS CHILDREN

This poem that was written by me at the end of 2014 has become the official poem of the Pan African Federalist Movement of which I am an active member since 2015 and which has committees all over the world

This call comes from deep within

From the depths of time, from eternity...

From the depths of tormented times

From the bottom of bruised, bloody centuries...

And of all the years of sovereignty being violated...

Africa is calling YOU, yes YOU, YOU and YOU again...

ALL OF US

Come, she says.

YOU my children, come to deliver me

Don't let me be mistreated, pillaged, bent...

Don't let me be raped,

Don't let me be grinded, bribed no more,

Come to me, to me my dearest children

Those who are close to me

Those who are far away, but close to my soul...

Those who are lost in the cold meanderings of the enemy...

Those who are righteous, those who are traitors, those who are vile...

Those who are tired, haggard, exsanguinated and only want to sleep...

Wake up, wake up

Get back to you

STAND UP my children STAND UP!

Come to the source of my Humanity

Come and recharge your batteries in my deep roots

Come regenerate yourself in my ancestral spirituality

Come and sit by my sacred fire...

Come in the shade of my bountiful nature

I am Mother Earth and I am abundance.

My breasts are still young and my milk is still luscious...

My waterfalls gush refreshingly intoxicating

My gems shine deep in all my cavities

All this will finally be yours, because I've been saving some for you...

My wealth is limitless despite all the looting...

My wealth is your great strength in spite of slavery.

My wealth is your smile in spite of all the trials

My wealth is your beautiful soul in spite of the perversions

You are IMMENSIVE BEINGS

Dress up at last in your magnificence

Take your power back

I'm waiting for YOU, My hope is in US...

STAND UP my children STAND UP free from all chains

START THE AFRICAN RENAISSANCE, EACH, ALL, TOGETHER, UBUNTU, UNITED, AT LAST !!!

Mame Hulo

http://etatsafricainsunis.org/

African Humanism, the concept of UBUNTU: "I am because we are".

In order to make this dream of unity come true, an exceptional concept is available, stemming from our ancestral wisdom, this is the concept of UBUNTU which originates in the Bantu languages.

Ubuntu means "I am because we are" or "I am what I am, thanks to what we all are". Someone from Ubuntu is open and available to others, because he or she is aware of belonging to something greater.

Let's say that it is an African social and human responsibility that includes all human beings, including criminals against humanity!

Hence this demand for the restoration of Harmony within Humanity with a concept of reparation and not of sanctions and punishment of criminals.

Here is European humanism according to Frantz Fanon, in Les Damnés de la terre (1961): "*This Europe that never stopped talking about men, never stopped proclaiming that it was only concerned about men, we know today what suffering Humanity has paid for each of the victories of its spirit.* "

Here are some articles extracted from THE MANDEN'S CHARTER or Charter of Kouroukan Fouga of 1222 in the Empire of Mali :

In terms of universal humanism, Africa is the first since 1222, to have proclaimed a Universal Declaration of Human Rights through **the Manden Charter or Charter of Kouroukan Fouga** in the Empire of Mali.

Article 1 : *"Every [human] life is life. It is true that one life appears in existence before another life. But a life is no more "ancient", no more respectable than another life. Just like one life is not superior to another life."*

Article 2 : *"Since every life is life, any harm done to a life requires reparation. Therefore, let no one attack his neighbour with impunity, let no one harm his neighbour, let no one cause harm to his fellow man. "*

Article 5 : *"Hunger is not a good thing; slavery is not a good thing; there is no greater calamity than these things. In this world, as long as we have the quiver and the bow, hunger will not kill anyone in the Manden, should famine ever strike. War will never again destroy a village on the Manden to take slaves. That means that no one will ever again put the bit in the mouth of his fellow man to sell it. Nor will anyone be beaten, let alone put to death because he is the son of a slave. "*

Article 6 : *"The essence of slavery is extinguished from this day on "from wall to another wall" of the Manden. The raid is banned from this day on in the Manden. Torments born of these horrors are ended from this day on the Manden. What*

147

an ordeal torment is, especially when the oppressed have no recourse. What a decay that slavery is! The slave enjoys no consideration anywhere in the world."

Let's go back to our ancestral African wisdom !

LET US DEMAND REPARATION !

Lanzistisman for a global repair in Reunion Island

By Philippe Bessière

For the Komité Rényoné Panafrikin & MIR Réunion

Franswa Sintomèr left us way too soon[12]. He was known, among other talents, as a creator of words. He thus created the concept of lanzistisman, which translation is nearly impossible, but which can be understood by the periphrase of a refoundation on the basis of justice. It is the slow, but deep down progress of this demand that we will try to trace. The idea of reparation for past crimes first imposed itself in the private sphere, involving the psychological after-effects, the transgenerational traumas. But we know that we cannot take justice into our own hands. Individual voices then became more numerous and more vehement, leading to demands. The issue then became a social one, involving trade unionists. But the complexity of the problems raised, and their lack of ownership by academic and political institutions, discouraged collective social action. It is indeed the role of the politician to take care of the polis (the city).

---

[12] Portrayed by Gilles GERARD, *Franswa Sintomer, lo maronèr. Les combats d'un militant culturel réunionnais, (fights of cultural activitist from Reunion Island)* préface de Mark, Nadia et Sharl Saint-Omer, Paris, L'Harmattan, 2017, 118 p.

The lyrical declaration of Paul Vergès in the Senate was not followed up[13].

It is by developing an ambitious project with all the parties concerned that we can hope to respond to Franswa's appeal. The purpose of this article is to present, without embellishment, the state of the issue of "reparations for the crimes of the slave trade and slavery" in Reunion Island, following as faithfully as possible its itinerary, without omitting the obstacles and pitfalls encountered along the way.

Reparation through history or the construction of historical awareness.

Shortly after the events that accompanied the 150th anniversary of the abolition of slavery in the French colonies, the school history curriculum was revised. At the congress of the FSU (Fédération Syndicale Unitaire, the majority among secondary school teachers), I defended a motion of regionalist inspiration:

"Since the beginning of the 2000 school year, an adaptation has been made to enable children to learn some of 'local history'. While the intention may seem praiseworthy, it turns

---

[13] A well-known declaration from Paul Vergès : « We are a people born out of a crime against humanity». This speech was made at the Senate and may be found in *Témoignages* (25 th/26th march 2000). Paul Vergès was acting as both the President of the Reunion Communist Party and the Alliance (a cartel of political parties and leading figures) and the Reunion District.

out that this concept has no consistency whatsoever, which consequently, arise new problems. So,

The study of mother civilizations continues to focus on Eurocentrism. In particular, Africa and Madagascar are evacuated, which does not allow us to understand the colonization process.

The history of the island is still only used as a pretext, which prohibits any coherence.

Studying the slave trafficking is only optional while it should be at the centre of the problematics.

Links between the regional and the national are not made explicit, the emphasis being deliberately placed on abolitionism.

In practice, few resources have been made available. In particular, the absence of a manual is to be deplored. On the other hand, there is no significant place given to "local history" during school examinations.

Proposals.

Regional history must be recognized as such with its own coherence and a timetable must be set for it. It should no longer be considered as a handicap, but as an asset to enable :

The dialogue between cultures of origin as exercised in the island. The knowledge of the cultural creolization process.

The affirmation of a regional personality as a response to the identity crisis affecting schooling and development.

The opening up to the geographical region as a preparation

to genuine regional cooperation.

A new relationship with the Metropolis in which the Region would regain its role as an actor. Regional history must be linked to national and international history.

A pedagogy of reparation for the serious harm caused by the slave trade, servile slavery and racism[14]. "

Twenty years after the failure of this motion, nothing has changed in National Education. Every teacher is doing as he or she pleases. The transfer rules have not changed. A generation of Reunion Islanders has been "educated" in ignorance and lies. They ask us today: Kisa nou lé ? [15] "We grew up learning about the history of France, but almost nothing about the history of our island. Beyond the beautiful postcards and tourist advertisements that I regularly saw in the corridors of the Parisian metro, I discovered over the course of my research that Reunion Island hides a heavy past, which traces left even today[16]. This generation nourishes a feeling of revolt for having been taught in

---

[14] Motion submitted according to the New Reunionese school trend, which gathered 19 votes in favour, 25 votes against it, 10 abstentions and one rejection. The FSU historic leader, Raymond Mollard, for Unity and Action and also Regional Adviser for Paul Vergès Alliance, having declared that they did not find enough time to think about it. The conference was held at Sainte Marie in December 2000.

[15] Kisa nou lé – Reflections on the Reunionese identity, a film of Sebastian CLAIN, 2019, 123 mn, video-on-demand brochure

[16] www.film-documentaire.fr, consulted 9/03/2020.

concealment and deception. Mr. Macron should be concerned about an "anti-French sentiment" among a growing number of young Reunionese. "

In September and October 2003, the Rasine Kaf association organized a series of conferences and debates throughout the island on the subject of reparations due for slavery and the slave trade. The opening in Saint-Paul was devoted to history. Indeed, without this knowledge, these claims, however legitimate they may be, cannot be substantiated. My speech provided an overview of several countries at the forefront of this struggle. Then I wondered about the ideological armament capable of carrying this demand and giving it the strength it sorely lacks.

"The only path that opens up prospects is that of a social, democratic and modern movement capable of investing itself in the cultural as well as the social and political fields, without giving up its independence. A movement capable of combining personal and group freedom, capable of dialogue with other components. The name that seems to impose itself almost by itself for this movement is cafritude, considering that negritude was a response to the slave trade, but that it did not answer the cafre[17] question.

---

[17] « One doesn't talk about negroes » in the Indian ocean where the slave trade began as far as the VIIIth century. « Cafres » are the slaves that have been snatched from the African continent, but there were also « Malbars » taken from the southern area of India, « Malagasy » people and « Malaysian » people who were enslaved. Moreover, there were also a substantial contingent of African people enrolled.

Cafritude will have to be stoic to face history. It should not spare any religion or power. It will have to be completely disenchanted and for this reason (if one follows Max Weber) completely modern. It will aim at repairing humanism and in order to do that, it will try to assert Cafres historical rights.

From a broken past, we do not want to make a broken horizon. The real reparation is the one that applies to the future. The slaves who fought for freedom would not deny this. They bequeath to us this motto: the duty of freedom![18] "

However, what was missing from my proposal was the means to build this historical consciousness. Ideology, philosophy about history, is not enough to unite a collective. It is necessary to reconnect the present with its origins, to understand the causal chains that have constituted it. This is necessary in order to recover continuity and to be able to give meaning. And in doing so, colonial history is unmasked because it is based on the principle that the colonized have no history. The certainties and values resulting from domination (mental in this case) are called into question. Hence a start, a new reading, a reappropriation of history. "Regional history" is not capable of making this radical break. Only pan-African history is consistent with this approach. Hence the importance of rereading the theses formulated over the past 50 years by Sheik Anta Diop: "It is

---

[18] Philippe BESSIERE, « Reunion Island : what kind of reparation ? », 20/09/2003 conference at Saint-Paul 20/09/2003 for the conferences-debate cycle « *Démounaz lesklavaz* : what kind of reparation ? » organized by *Rasine Kaf* association.

not a question of creating from scratch a history more beautiful than that of others, so as to morally boost the people during the period of struggle for independence, but of **starting from the obvious idea that each people has a history.** What is indispensable for a people to better direct its evolution is to know its origins, whatever they may be. If by any chance our story is more beautiful than we expected, this is only a happy detail that should no longer bother us as soon as we have provided enough objective evidence to support it." (...) "The people realize what is solid and valid in their own cultural and social structures, in their thinking in general; they also realize what has consequently not stood the test of time. They discover the real extent of their borrowings, they can now define themselves in a positive way from indigenous criteria that are not imagined, but real. They have a new awareness of their values and can now define their cultural mission, not passionately, but objectively; for they see better the cultural values that they are best able, given their state of evolution, to develop and bring to other peoples[19]."

And after a one more time reading, what remains is to adapt their reuse to another era, and in different historical and geographical scales. And starting undoubtedly from this simple proposition, capable of putting history back in its place: Reunion Island is not part of French history, but it is France that came to make history on an African island.

---

[19] Cheik Anta DIOP, *Nations nègres et culture,* Paris, Présence africaine, 1954, pp 9-10 et p. 19.

Religious reparation.

The responsibility of the Catholic Church was clearly stated by Reynolds Michel:

"The duty of reparation is imposed on the Church by virtue of her own moral theology once she accepts her responsibility. Hence the commitment of the Christian Churches in South Africa to the struggle for reparation. For without reparation and economic development there is, they say, no reconciliation.

The fact that the Church in Reunion has decided to bring its contribution in asking that slavery be declared a "crime against humanity" (Mgr. Gilbert Aubry) implies, it seems to us, that it agrees to make its contribution to the reparation of this crime by fully assuming its moral responsibility. In any case, this is my wish.

In Mauritius, a group of priests recently took the initiative to launch a National Movement for Reparations (MNPR), as part of the international campaign of reparation movements. The great mass of Creoles, descendants of slaves, bear the multiple consequences of what is being described as a "crime against humanity" by the Office of the United Nations High Commissioner for Human Rights.

Hence, they say, this movement is aiming to inform, sensitize, raise awareness, give energy to the whole of Mauritian society to work towards carrying out an act of justice for the descendants of slaves" (Declaration of 8 August 2003).

"Reparation can take many forms. It is not only economic,

as has been said here and there. The Church can find its place alongside other living forces in this country to make its own contribution to this reparation by articulating it in a work of remembrance and mourning. It can already begin by highlighting names of the slaves who worked on the construction of our cathedrals alongside Monnet, Levavasseur, Joffard, Scubilion and others, and make its contribution to the financing of projects in the neighbourhoods where the majority of those who suffer most from the after-effects of slavery are to be found, in view to get to a better living together for all components of Reunionese society[20]. "

It should be said that the diocese has not embarked on this path. This defection, following that of political parties, weighs heavily on the public lock on the issue of reparations due for the slave trade and slavery. The same effect comes true within the Inter-religious Group including Hindus, Jews, Catholics and Muslims. Like the Catholic Church, Islam has responsibilities in the Indian Ocean slave trade. All are concerned by the demonization of animism and ancestor worship.

---

[20] Reynolds Michel, « Church and Slavery : what kind of reparation ? », communication issued at Sainte-Suzanne on 11 october *2003*, during the conferences-debate « *Démounaz lesklavaz* : what kind of reparation ? » organized by *Rasine Kaf* association. Reynolds Michel is a catholic priest, a former CDPS leader , who became the founder of EPI (Entente Pour l'Interculturel).

The MIARO[21] association is the first to militate to take the cult of Malagasy[22] ancestors out of its confinement in private courtyards and practice ceremonies in the open and open to all. Since 2004, on the Dimitile[23] plateau, Atidamba has been celebrated, "*a ritual that aims to honour the memory of Malagasy ancestors resting in Reunion Island as well as that of all the fugitives who received neither funeral honours nor burial, by covering with a white shroud the stele dedicated to Queen Sarlava, King Laverdure and the watchman Dimitile, symbols of the resistance of fugitives to the slave trade and slavery[24].*" MIARO also claims the establishment of a place of worship in the lower part of the island, also dedicated to information on practices and the dissemination of Malagasy culture.

Generally speaking, African spirituality should be taught, which is what Kolektif Vanina Galais-Férard[25] proposes to do by organizing a school for which it is asking support from elected officials. The kolektif has undertaken a tour of the

---

[21] Malagasy polysemous word with three meanings « defend », « bring value », « mix up with »

[22] *servis zansèt* in Reunion Island usually mingle African and Malagasy rituals to ancestor worship.

[23] Dimitile means « watchman » in malagasy. The leading black resisters were the ones who would be responsible for that.

[24] 7lameslamer.net, consulted on 9/03/2020.

[25] From the name of a young woman assassinated in may 2018. He mother Noëline, is the one who initiated *Kolektif* in order to fight not only women killers but any kind of violence engendered by the cultural loss and the breakdown of the reunionese society.

island of town halls to raise awareness about its project[26].

Religious resistance to slavery has played a very important role in restoring a sacred space to the person, preserving ritual gestures and beliefs that have been transmitted to us. The syncretism of practices has produced a popular[27] religion that is a rich heritage and an essential resource in the reconquest of identity.

Psychological repair.

The journalist Estéfany reported in Témoignages of 1st June 2004 on an inter-associative forum on victimology held in Saint-Denis on 21 and 22 May 2004. On the subject of reparation for slavery, Jean-Loup Roche, psychologist and vice-president of ARIV (Reunion Island branch of the Institute of Victimology) raised the problem of intra-family and neighbourhood violence: "*I have verified through my work that young offenders are very often deprived of their fathers. They may be physically present, without providing any support to their children. So, there is a lack of a stable male reference point and the assertion then goes through the transgressive mode.* "Estéfany continued: "*When a victim has no resilience, no reference point, no help to help him overcome his suffering, he may enter into a process of*

---

[26] Noëline Férard Interview in *Témoignages* march 7th, 2020.

[27] Prosper ÈVE, *Popular religion in La Réunion,* Institute of Linguistics and Anthropology, Reunion Island University, 1985, 167 p.

'overvictimisation', linked to a painful collective history, that of slavery (testimonies at the forum confirmed this)."

This observation is in line with the much more explicit statement made by Jean-Pierre Cambefort, who has eighteen years of experience in special education in Reunion Island as an educational psychologist, during a conference-debate organized by Rasine Kaf: "*The slave, as he is not a person, as his name was changed, (...) and has no longer has any lineage ties with his descendants. That's a very important issue to me, with heavy consequences on the psychological organization of the family. The father no longer has the right to pass on his name. As the Black Code specifies, the father no longer has the right to recognize his children. This for me has enormous consequences. It means that in the family organization, parental images, father and mother are no longer complementary. Men no longer transmit what is called symbolic capital, that is to say, symbolic roots, the language, the ancestors' memory, to their children. They no longer represent vis-à-vis their children the parent who is a third party in the relationship between mother and child. And men are (this is extremely important) also ousted from their capacity to reproduce [by the violence of commanders, masters or white people passing by]*[28]*. All these children were in fact the result of a*

---

[28] I am taking the liberty to change the speech of Jean-Pierre Cambefort that I have reported myself in writing. As a matter of fact, it talks about « the race bastardisation that has been made possible by commanders who put the real fathers aside ». On the one hand, one doesn't know which fathers we're talking

violence called "attack of filiation". Paternity was prevented, the image of the father and that of manhood was not transmitted[29]. "And to conclude that "reparation also requires the restoration of the family[30]."

It is understandable that psychology alone is far from sufficient for a task of this magnitude. To solve a societal problem, all institutions must be mobilized. And in order to make that happen, it would be advisable that, after having been victims of history, the Reunionese born out of slavery should not become also victims of the denial of history, as Estéfany pointed it out in the press article quoted above: "Do not shut yourself up in a fatalistic vision, underpinned by the denial of history. (...) When the problem of the recognition of the history of slavery in Reunion Island is pointed out, we must stop looking at the finger to the detriment of the problem[31]."

---

about and on the other hand, it seems that the fact that commanders also were black slaves is not taken into account. This point outlines, a word from maloya corroborates what Jean-Pierre Cambefort was denouncing : « *Marizane lété mon fanm / Komanèr la fini ralé / Na lé rodé, na lé rodé / Na lé rodé in fanm pou twé !* » My translation : « Marie-Jeanne was my wife / But the commander took her for himself / We'll go and get/We'll go and get/ We'll go and get you another wife ! »

[29] *Démounaz lesklavaz* : What kind of reparations ? A cycle of four conference-debate organized by Rasine Kaf

[30] *Témoignages* (Testimonies) 29th september 2003.

[31] *Témoignages (Testimonies)* 1st june 2004 : « A Victim of history or of its denial ? » We would say « a victim of history and of its denial ».

The problem of the functional dysfunctions of families and the intergenerational transmission provoked has been thoroughly analyzed by Ghislaine Bessière: "the Reunionese society functions according to codes: the man of marrying age must first seek shelter prior to found his family, in the same way that the Comorian man needs to build his banga to live his sexuality. It is he who must bring the money home and feed his family. This function being entrusted to the man, most of the young people of the working class can no longer assume it, simply because the conditions are no longer met to allow him to be in adequacy with his deep culture and his moral duty.

And the necessary conditions for living as a couple and flourishing are not met when cohabitation between generations becomes an obligation rather than a choice. The access to the building of a family is barred, roles often reversed between mother and daughter as regards the children education ; the father, often forced to delegate his role to the eldest, is thus evading his own responsibility.

This forced cohabitation is one of the consequences of isolated motherhood, as women are forced to remain in their families of origin in order to be able to bring up their children, especially in the case of early pregnancies, which are still numerous in the Reunion Island. The depreciation of the parental image caused by this situation, in which the father is seen as the son and the grandfather as the father, necessarily leads to a confusion of roles that is detrimental to the child. Although physically present, the father is perceived as not in charge, absent from his paternal function, more precisely, the mother sometimes acting like a mother and sometimes like a daughter, provokes the same ambiguity in the child's mind, who will be constantly testing his parents legitimacy.

We find ourselves there, confronted with a permanent after-effect of slavery, and in particular of the Black Code, which institutes paternity for the master, since he, and he alone, has the power over the woman's children: if she is free, her children will be free; if she is a slave, her children will be slaves. However, the status of freedom is granted by the master, who decides who he can set free, according to which services were provided[32].

This question of who is the master of the house still arises regularly in the household, when violence replaces the function of authority. Hurt, violence and destruction are still the lot of a number of men who, by losing authority over their families, have lost their sense of behavior and the reference point they represent for their children. When the child doubts his father, he is led to imagine himself as a bastard; the bastard being the one who has a mother, but no recognized father, no father present. The bastard is not the half-breed, although he may have been born of a union between two nasyon, the term "nation" corresponding, in Reunion Island, to a cultural and biological component of the Reunionese population.

---

[32] The request for emancipation is made by the master to colonial authorities, according to his will.

Being born without a father means being defenceless, or having to relegate his protection to another male figure found in the mother's family side. It can also be the brother, the dada[33], or any other male figure who can take on the role of guide. The referent may also be someone from the street: in this case we speak of a big brother, although this notion of big brother is nowadays[34] fading away."

Social redress.

From the trade union point of view, which is in the field of demands, this is not a promising theme. The sectors of society most affected by the after-effects of slavery are not unionized even though they would have had access to non-precarious employment if they were. Labour unions have never succeeded in organizing the unemployed, if they really have had the will to do so. In Reunion Island, members of the poor civil society are not represented. They are downgraded, relegated and stigmatized to the point where they too often express only urban violence outbursts.

At the initiative of the Rasine Kaf association, and under the patronage of the Association for the House of Civilizations

---

[33] A replacement of the father, when needed, chosen within the family (close family or extended family), however the foster father or the priest cannot be chosen.

[34] Ghislaine BESSIÈRE, « *Lanzistisman* pour un avenir réunionnais », « Lanzistisman for a reunionese future » a non published paper september 2019, 6 p.

and Unity of Reunion Island, a social and cultural forum was held in the town of Le Port on 13 and 14 December 2003[35]. Speakers included the historian Prosper Ève ("Commemoration and duty of remembrance") and secretaries general of the CGTR, Georges-Marie Lépinay ("The conditions for the exercise of democracy in Reunion") and Ivan Hoarau ("Regional space and development issues"). In the absence of planters, the agrarian issue was just briefly raised. The broader problem of access to land for social tenants could not be addressed either.

However, the issue of land reform has recently been revived by Christiane Taubira, who called for a distribution of lands (belonging to the State) in favour of the descendants of Guyanese slaves. Ghislaine Bessière proposes to "*reflect on this proposal and extend it to the descendants of engaged people, those who had a colonial status and who worked the land for a hundred years or more without benefiting from ownership of the land. We must start from the fundamental principle that the land belongs to those who worked on it, and today we can claim the land for the ti plantèr, a claim that dates from the 1970s in Reunion Island.*

The land reform is in fact an indispensable issue that we must address. To do that, it is necessary to make an inventory of all the fallow ground, especially those belonging to Sucreries de Bourbon, a land that was inherited from the colonial plantation and that a redistribution (possibly through

---

[35] *Témoignages (Testimonies)* du 11 décembre 2003.

shareholding) be considered. But it is also necessary to reflect on the monoculture of sugar cane, and move from the sugar cane plantation to a diversified agriculture in order to feed the people of Reunion who still depend too much on imports.

Achieving food self-sufficiency is the objective in the short and medium term in order to enable the population to get out of the spiral of dependence, to promote multi culture and methods conducive to the protection of the planet, in particular permaculture and tree planting. Stop the use of glyphosate, for a reasoned agriculture, would enable to definitively turn the page from slavery and housing[36] to a system of family production or agricultural cooperatives, perhaps based on the example of Africa. Planters need to see their nurturing role and their pride[37] restored."

Financial compensation.

" When slavery was abolished, slaveowners received what was called colonial compensation from the State in the amount of 711.59 francs per slave. For big slaveowners, this sum was given to them in vouchers from the Banque de la Réunion, created in 1851. The history of the BR is directly linked to the history of slavery, since it was created from

---

[36] Malcom FERDINAND, *Decolonized and friendly environment. Thinking ecology from the caribbean world,* Paris, Seuil, 2019, 456 p.

[37] Ghislaine BESSIÈRE, September 2019 paper previously quoted.

funds allocated as compensation for the loss of slaves[38]. "

"The issue of financial reparations must be addressed, although it seems to me today quite difficult to determine exactly who is a descendant of slaves and who is not. To do so, DNA testing is needed to find out who still has "black blood" in their veins. The problem must be posed more effectively in terms of managing the amount of black blood that each Reunionese possesses within him, and the balance, or even why not, the harmony that he is able to establish between all these amounts. This problem is not only metaphysical since we know what consequences are involved in denying oneself and erasing one's origins in the construction and blossoming of one's own identity. Undertaking individual financial reparations therefore seems risky and would only reinforce historical falsification of family alliances and genealogies[39]. "

However, there may be other solutions than individual compensation: *"We all know that the Banque de la Réunion was taken over today by the Caisse d'Épargne. It had been created with the money from compensation payments to owners. This financial windfall must be accounted for today, to be reused in reparation by redistributing compensation benefits to the descendants of slaves. We demand that the descendants of slaves be able to benefit from the*

---

[38] Statement from Sudel Fuma reported by le *Journal de l'Ile de la Réunion* on 7 th avril 2004.

[39] Ghislaine BESSIERE, « What's the program for public reparations? », december 2003, paper non published.

inheritance of the work of their ancestors. The free work they performed for 134 years, from 1714[40] to 1848, must be valued taking into account the price of paid work at the time and according to the number of hours. This money will be put into a comprehensive reparation program, managed by the public authorities and under citizens control. Which will avoid individual financial compensation, but allow a controlled and managed redistribution as part of a public reparations policy[41]. "

Cultural repairs.

As a wave of protesters centred on purchasing power swept through the DOM, Reunion's cultural activists formed the "Kiltir Partou" collective to put forward their demands. The "History, Memory, Heritage and Toponymy" commission reported on its work on 23 March 2009 in the Port. Here are large extracts from this report which was validated by applause.

"The central idea of the platform is based on the principle of Reparation, which we are declaring under the form of concrete demands affecting all social, educational, cultural and economic spheres."

---

[40] Date on which the Black Code related to France and Bourbon islands was recorded (Mauritius and Reunion Island).

[41] Ghislaine BESSIÈRE, 2019 paper, previously quoted.

History, a fundamental right.

The first demand concerns the Right to History, which we consider to be a fundamental right. In this respect, we have highlighted the need to develop the means for each and every Reunionese, whatever their age and social condition, to have access to the history of their country.

The teaching of history. This involves learning history from kindergarten to university, but also through the development of research programs and actions carried out by the University, by associations or by the individual himself.

The appropriation of history requires knowledge of it. This knowledge must be facilitated by making available to the public the means of knowledge such as books, genealogical records, etc. These tools must be developed by public authorities and associations, and made available in school and public libraries, archives, and within associations that develop these openings to knowledge.

The repatriation of all archives on Reunion Island. To this end, archives on slavery, engagementism and colonization must be repatriated to Reunion Island and brought together in the Departmental Archives Office of Reunion Island, whether in the form of copies, microfilms or other digital media.

Pre-emption of original historical documents. Documents related to Reunion's heritage, which are the subject of auctions, and particularly old books and originals, must be paid into public funds, in particular through pre-emptions.

Preventive archaeology and archaeological research.

All historic sites must be listed and archaeological research carried out so that their historic character can be confirmed: slave cemeteries, runaways camps, public places of worship (sapèl malbar, Catholic temples, doany, etc.), enlisted men's camps, traditional villages.

The classification of these historic sites is one of the fundamental conditions for their preservation. Road or urban development projects must respect these historic sites and places of worship. The population must be systematically consulted before any development project that concerns its immediate environment involving its land and cultural heritage. (...)

Heritage inventory

All historical sites must be listed and classified. They must be safeguarded and rehabilitated. Heritage objects relating to slavery, runaways, indentured labour and colonization must be identified and preserved. Public information on objects found in different sites of the island by associations, individuals or institutions in charge of heritage preservation such as the DRAC, the Region, the Department must be disseminated as soon as possible.

These objects found during development works, personal or institutional research or in the framework of projects implemented by associations must be listed, dated and transferred to the common heritage. Such is the case of the bones found in the Phaonce cave by the ONF, in Dimitile by the association Capitaine Dimitile, and in Saint-Paul during cyclone Firinga. Objects found in Tapcal by explorers, objects collected by the GRAHTER[42] in Salazie, chains of the Desbassayns prison. The museum of Villèle must be completed by the slave section, their census, but also all their working tools, as well as objects of abuse and restraint.

The toponymy.

The Parc National des Hauts must investigate on the issue of fugitives and freedom, and thus rehabilitate the memory of the Hauts area. It is its duty to contribute to the safeguarding of the ways of life and cultural heritage still in use in the circuses and in the Hauts area. Other public authorities have the same duty with regard to some villages situated in the Bas area, such as Grande-Chaloupe... Taking an interest solely in the fauna and flora seems to us to be far from enough in view of the rich history of the Hauts area of the island, which foundation is based on the epic, of fugitives and their counterpart, fugitives hunters, as well as many exchanges that took place between kivis (the poor white people who escaped the slavery system by appropriating land in the Hauts area (Cilaos, Salazie, Mafate) and fugitives.

---

[42] Archaeology and History Research Organization in Reunion Island conducted for a long time by Marc Kichenapanaïdou, a pioneer in the field of archaeology in the Reunion Island.

For an immediate rebalancing of street names and public squares. There are still too many streets named after former slaveowners or people who founded the slave system, such as Jacob de la Haye, Colbert (who conceived the black code), General Decaen (who established the Decaen code), the Indies company, the name of Desbassayns in several towns in Reunion Island, etc. We ask for an immediate rebalancing and a renaming of the streets in order to introduce in the city the names of the slaves, fugitives and committed men who contributed to the construction of Reunion Island. In the similar way, public figures such as political activists, trade unionists, cultural actors who fought for democracy must find their place in the city. We must refer to our own heroes in the history of Reunion Island and give them the place they duly deserve.

Ideological repair

Debates held in *Kiltir Partou*, however, revealed a great deal of duplicity. For instance, this introduction by Axel Gauvin, writer and activist for the Creole language, president of *Lofis la Lang*: "*The word reparation really bothers me!*[43] " In fact, his position is in line with the practice of a whole fringe of the cultural movement that refuses to do a work on memory,

---

[43] April 19th 2009 at Port.

that dissociates their claim for the language from that of history[44].

The rest of the discussion is quite a real eye-opener:

"To whom will be asked any compensation for the damage?"

"It's up to the French state to repair!" Obviously. But social relations, property regimes, mentalities and representations: These matters also need to be repaired !

In another debate, the historian Laurent Hoarau had the opportunity to castigate the hypocrisy of elected officials. "The UNESCO Charter was signed by the association of mayors. Since then, Grand-Bois and Dampierre have been wiped off. I ser pa ryin alé kri si governman fransé si nou isi nou fé ryin![45] "This is where the reality lies : within the contempt of the so-called "educated" classes for popular culture, and within the desire to make invisible any traces of what is euphemistically called "a painful history". This cleavage between the French and the Reunionese can be found within the Creole world, inside living rooms and in the rural world. Inherited from the cascade of contempt during the hardest times of colonialism, the habitus inhabits

---

[44] In my paper released on decembre 2002, « Histoire et créolité », 6 p., which remained on line for quite a long time on the following site <potomitan.info>.

[45] Statements held at Saint-Paul on may 25th 2009. Grand-Bois is a former sugar factory. Dampierre is a *malbar chapel*. « There's no need to claim anything before the French government if Reunionese people despise their own history ! »

bodies[46], manners, levels of language, looks...

The claim for recognition has to deal with arrogant paternalism or superb indifference. When it does not face various kinds of discrimination. We will give just two examples. The first concerns lazarettos where those arriving from a ship infected with a contagious disease were quarantined. The troops lazaretto has been rehabilitated and upgraded by the Department. The slave lazaretto has fallen into ruin and is closed to the public, no demonstrations can be held there any longer. Second scornful treatment: large subsidies are given for Chinese or Hindu festivals, but none for Africa Day. We get a curt reply: "You have December 20!"That's it, for them, Africa equals slavery. 171 years later, they don't want to give up on that...

But institutions are not the only ones concerned. There are those elected representatives who just settle with fine declarations in Paris, but do nothing on the ground. There are those trade unionists who admit that Kaf has been the most exploited, but who do not propose anything to change their situation today. And there are those associations that have no scruples about diverting resources intended for Afrodescendence to use them for other purposes. And the worst thing in this game of fools is that when we denounce these manifest abuses, abuses of dominant positions,

---

[46] Prosper ÈVE, *Le corps des esclaves de l'île Bourbon. Histoire d'une reconquête*, Paris-Sorbonne, PUPS, 2013, 524 p.

abuses of weakness, we, Kaf associations, are the ones accused of acting racist.

Like all dominated groups, reparation for the descendants of the victims of slavery must first be made through speaking out, otherwise the silence of some of them will continue to cover the noise made by of others. These dominant groups have no qualms about speaking up for subordinates. They rightfully fear everything the dominated have to say. The younger generation might be the one that will finally utter the big Kaf scream that will put everyone back to their rightful place. It already has its representatives in the person of Socko lo Kaf[47].

Conclusion

In a permanent way, we find again the theme of wandering[48], which constitutes the red thread of a historical condition, and which has repercussions in every field. "*What Alain Lorraine called social cafritude[49], to show that*

---

[47] His poem can be read in Marcel DORIGNY book, *Arts and Letters against slavery,* introduced by Maryse CONDÉ, Paris, Cercle d'Art, 2018, 240 p.

[48] As far as inclusion in the city is concerned read our study : RASINE KAF, *Itinérances,* report delivered to Reunion Island Region in september 2008, non published, 2 vol., 133 p. et 77 p.

[49] We'd rather name it « cafrity » to describe an inherited condition, something already there and maintain « cafritude » for speaking up and being aware of this condition. To use a well-known formulation of Freud, our ambition is that from "that" we get to "I" . This can be made possible only from the uttering of a

cafritude has moved from the biological to the social, but is based on the same process of downgrading, the KAF always being the one who is excluded from society.

Analyzing this social permanence of exclusion means accepting to see how stigmas of slavery have become embedded in interstices of society to the point of hindering any effort at social emancipation. (...) These are all elements that must be taken into account today to build the foundations of true social justice, societal equilibrium and genuine development. What we can call **lanzistisman.**

In reparation are included all spheres of society in a mental, psychological, economic and financial dimension. It is both collective and individual. That is why we must launch an open debate on reparation. Why not set up a Truth and Reconciliation Commission as has been done in the Republic of South Africa?[50] Or Truth and Justice as in Mauritius (a voluminous report has been submitted, but we are still waiting for concrete decisions[51])? "Eight years have gone by without anything notable happening. "Some people obviously find this voluminous report thorny, not to say embarrassing, where the question of land ownership and

---

word and this word is « Kafre » already existing instead of a fake-self.

[50] Desmond TUTU, No future without forgiveness, translated from english (Afrique du Sud) by Josiane and Alain Deschamps, Paris, Albin Michel, 2000, 282 p.

[51] The Truth and Justice Commission, created in 2009 delivered its report in november 2011, with up to 300 recomendations included.

the review of cases of dispossession deemed fraudulent[52] appears very strongly. " Until Clency Harmon's hunger strike in April 2019, when the Mauritian government promised to set up a Land Court (a court competent to settle land disputes).

There is one thing we must always keep in mind: We do not have to wait for a repairman! Let us demand what is rightfully due to us, so that we can finally take our destiny in hand! Justice is also a struggle.

---

[52] *Le Mauricien* dated april 15, 2019.

AFRÈS, our identity and our common struggle

By Nita Brochant, Jaklin Jacqueray, Luc Reinette

The Editorial Committee of the CIPN

International Committee of Black Peoples

OUR ANCESTORS, OUR CARIBBEAN AND AMERICAN ANCESTORS OF AFRICAN ORIGIN, ARE AFRICANS WHO WERE REDUCED TO SLAVERY, AND WHOM WE HAVE DECIDED TO NAME AFRÈS ...

After decades of denials due to an alienation skilfully inculcated by Western specialists of oblivion, we have achieved independence of thought, independence of mind, which has enabled us to stop thinking as the other wants us to think, to stop owning his prejudices against us.

As far as we are concerned, we came out of their paradigm to create our own, we came out of the sphere of slavery though that characterizes the Western world and also, it must be said forcefully, the Arab-Muslim world that practiced 13 centuries of slavery of a rare barbarity towards our Ancestors.

Maya ANGELOU, by affirming that: *"I am the dream and the hope of the Slave"* refers us to both our identity and our mission, ours and that of the generations that will succeed us. We must then stop for a moment to reflect on this strong phrase that questions our human condition yesterday and today.

We must stop on this call to action of Maya ANGELOU at a time when reflection had not begun on the scope of the term "slave", but we must recognize the immense merit of having established the essential relationship of kinship with them, our filiation, and of having stated that we were **their dream and their hope**... Can we individually and collectively empty ourselves completely and transport ourselves into our past to think of ourselves as Africans deported and enslaved? Can we then, shackled and subjected to the worst abuses, in a world of relentless and murderous slavery, think of posterity, think of those who would be our descendants and who would one day avenge us for the humiliation and rehabilitate us in our full humanity?

Louis DELGRES, one of the heroes of the anti-slavery struggle in Guadeloupe, had declared in May 1802, shortly before blowing himself up with 350 of our brave grandparents rather than surrender to the French soldiers: *"Our names will survive on the Ocean of Ages. And others will come after us, who, happier, will conquer the freedom we have only glimpsed...".*

There is obviously a common thread between Maya ANGELOU thoughts, that of DELGRES and that of Frantz FANON who later declared that: *"Each generation must in a relative opacity discover its mission or betray it...".*

Moreover, some thinkers have rightly stated that *evil often triumphs only through the inaction of good people...* Physical inaction or intellectual inaction, which consists in thinking that things can remain as they are and that it is not useful to question or put into perspective an imposed statusquo.

Did we ask ourselves how the rest of the world looked at us, how the rest of the world looked at our world, the **Black World**? No one is allowed to be indifferent to it, because no one can live with dignity without a minimum of consideration for others and for oneself.

Whether or not they have practiced slavery, all other peoples, with very rare exceptions, still see in the Black Man, a descendant of a slave (sic) and therefore almost a slave (sic), a being who is part of a sub-humanity... and who deserves only contempt or indifference.

That is why we consider it essential to name ourselves and declare to the whole universe our identity, our strength and pride in being black, our satisfaction in being African or Afro-descendants.

Yes, Africa and Africans are the origin of the world. It has been now scientifically established that Africa is the cradle of Humanity, at the origin of literature, science, mathematics, the pyramids... **But Africa cannot and must not be considered as a matrix that disappears after giving life to Humanity**. By this we mean that the first men who populated the earth must not be sacrificed, condemned to disappear by the lack of conscience and consideration they would have for themselves. By the lack of demand they would have towards others, especially towards those who would have plundered the existence of their Ancestors, their parents and their own one, by practicing slavery, **whether transatlantic or trans-Saharan**, for centuries and without any excuse...

At this point the issue of reparations arises, which cannot be separated from the very notion of dignity. If we consider all men to be equal, whatever their ethnicity, we must consider that crimes and outrages committed by some of them against others *must be repaired* without the goodwill of perpetrators being taken into account . Only equity and justice must be taken into account. There can be no justice for one and another for the other, justice for whites made by whites and justice for blacks made by whites. This principle also applies to Arab-Muslim racists and their justice for black Africans.

As we have already said and repeated, **Reparations and Decolonization are consubstantial**, one cannot be realized without the other being realized at the same time. The state of most African or Caribbean nations that have become independent without Reparations is eloquent: **one cannot emerge unscathed from several centuries of spoliation and domination**, nor develop if the fundamental financial and material tools are not available. Otherwise, we open the way to neo-colonialism, a situation in which **we have no control** over anything. Here, the synonym of

Decolonization is **FREEDOM**, Freedom to think, Freedom to think about oneself, and most of all, the freedom to assume one's destiny without any guardianship, be it political or spiritual .

There is also the essential notion of Respect which can only be concretized through a process and a requirement of Rehabilitation of our Ancestors: the process of rehabilitation, **it is up to us and to us alone** to do it within the framework of self-repair. As for the requirement of rehabilitation, we must formulate it in the direction of all other peoples who *designate us as they wish, without worrying for a moment how we feel about the words and expressions* they use to designate or represent us...

Sometimes, unaware of the weight of words, some Western and even African or Afro-descendant writers, journalists or politicians, though declared anti-colonialists, indulge in unbearable writings or remarks, evoking *millions of African slaves* deported to America. Writing this is to disregard or deny the fact that these millions of human beings deported in inhuman conditions were **People**, our **Fathers and Mothers**; they were artisans, fishermen, hunters, sculptors, dignitaries, bearers of a several thousand years old civilization.

With regard to these people, whether they are writers, journalists or politicians, conscious or unconscious of the stakes and the weight of words, **we must demand** that they no longer call our Ancestors "Slaves", but that from now on they respect them by naming them ENSLAVED AFRICANS, ENSLAVED AFRICAN ANCESTORS (for their descendants) or AFRES... No, we are not from slaves descent!

In our country, renowned intellectuals such as Hélène MIGEREL or Gladys DEMOCRITE, artists such as Marie-Line DAHOMAY or Luc-Hubert SEJOR are doing a remarkable job to give its letters of nobility to the concept of AFRES which constitutes, as Hélène MIGEREL said, an act of independence of thought ...

Wherever we have been transplanted throughout the world, we, as Afro-descendants should erect steles and monuments in memory of these Ancestors whose dream and hope were in us, and work at the level of international bodies to establish an **International Day of Rehabilitation, as a corollary of Reparations, a non-negotiable demand**...

Thus will gradually begin a new era where the image of our Ancestors and therefore our image and the image of Blacks in the World will be restored and respected .

AFRÈS is the clamour of the Dignity found again as Mrs. MIGEREL says it so well.

Our Honour and the happiness of our children is at stake, children of the Black World who are today so mistreated. And for whom we must fight so that tomorrow, like all the children of the world, they can live in **honour, dignity and prosperity, so that they can proudly follow in the footsteps of their Ancestors.**

In this Decade of People of African Ancestry, let us dare to accomplish our Mission.

Notes :

the word AFRES is used in the majority of languages of countries that have experienced slavery.

Hélène MIGEREL is a Doctor of Educational Sciences and Psychoanalyst.

Gladis DEMOCRITE is a lawyer.

REPARATIONS —An an urgent requirement for humanity

AFRÈS: Self-repair through the power of the verb "let us rehabilitate our enslaved African Ancestors by stopping calling them "slaves ! "

By Gladys Démocrite

Lawyer - CIPN Member

They come from over there, at the other side of the Ocean, from the distant Land of Africa, where their own Ancestors are resting... They themselves became Ancestors, after having suffered horrors of the slave trade, slavery and assimilation....

Today, few of their descendants have kept a link with them, because in the collective imagination, they belong to that abstract and impersonal mass that the word "slave" qualifies.

Even for us, their descendants, it is difficult for us to feel that we are talking about members of our family, our distant ancestors, when we refer to "slaves". The word, in itself, carries with it their induced references, its energy charge, its symbolic weight and its cultural (even identity) conditioning.

Being a slave is not an essence in itself. No one is born a slave. It is always an oppressor who forcibly imposes this status on a category of men and women. It is, moreover, the one who enslaves his victims who refers to them as "slaves". On the other hand, he who is enslaved always sees himself first and foremost as a man, not as a slave. When the enslaved man wants to talk about his family members, his children, his parents, his Ancestors, he does not refer to them as "slaves", because he knows that the word "slave" is not his identity, but a status imposed by the master.

Therefore, questioning the very term "slave", with all representations associated with it, seems to us essential to address the subject of reparations for crimes against humanity that constitute the transatlantic slave trade, slavery, colonization and assimilation. Indeed, one of the first acts of reparation should, in our view, be an act of self-repair that would question our relationship with our enslaved Ancestors. This would make it possible, for example, to find out whether, through the use of a word as common as "slave", we are not unconsciously participating in nurturing a collective imagination that cultivates the rejection of our Ancestors (and therefore the consequent rejection of ourselves).

Some may wonder why the word "slave" poses a problem, since this is how the French language refers to the victims of the slave trade and slavery.

But that is precisely the point, since the terms "slave" and "slavery" were chosen by those who thought up, organized, financed and regulated this hateful crime, by those who had our Ancestors captured, raided, deported, "enslaved", raped, tortured, reified, assimilated and creolized. "Slavery" is the word they chose to qualify in a watered-down way their appalling crime. Therefore, when they call our Ancestors "slaves", it is also with all the weight of their racist values and ideologies that they use this word.

However, for us, whose parents were directly victims of these crimes, should we apprehend our Ancestors with the same racist values as their executioners? Have we ever wondered who these African Ancestors are and what is the real relationship we have with those whom everyone likes to call "slaves"?

First of all, let us put ourselves in context, because the slave-owning period in Guadeloupe (from 1635 to 1794 and then from 1802 to 1848) was never peaceful and pacified. Numerous revolts and violent assaults were very regularly led by these African Ancestors against slave settlers. From the beginning of the French presence in Guadeloupe (in 1635), the resistance had been organized to the point that the first camp of "runaway negroes" was set up in 1636 (i.e. in the first year of presence on the territory).

Twenty years later, in 1656, the first large-scale revolt broke out and demonstrated the extent to which our Ancestors, even though they were scattered throughout all the dwellings of the country, were able to organize, communicate with each other and wage a real armed struggle in order to free themselves from the yoke of slavery and to take full possession of Guadeloupe.

Thus the historian of the time, Jean-Baptiste DUTERTRE, recounted the revolt of 1656:

"Two wicked negroes, one called Pedre, and the other Jean Le Blanc, secretly compelled (...) all the other negroes (...) to slaughter all the hut-masters, keep their wives, and create two Kings of their nation in the island, one in Basse-Terre, and the other one in Capesterre."

(*Jean-Baptiste DUTERTRE, " Histoire générale des Antilles habitées par les Français" (General History of West Indies inhabited by the French), tome I, p.500, 1667)*

The reality and the violence of those acts of resistance carried out at that time are well understood. One must be comprehend that European slavers had to reconquer the island militarily, with all the coercive and repressive means that one could imagine in order to preserve the interests of the colonists and the State. However, despite all the bloodshed, many decades later, the resistance of enslaved Africans never did waver.

So, in 1726, a Navy lieutenant wrote his report on the situation in Guadeloupe on the following terms:

"in Guadeloupe, more than 600 Negro fugitives huddled together in four bands are sending daily detachments of 60 to 80 men to plunder houses and despite the fact that there are continuously detachments of militia sent after them, we could not avoid thefts and abductions of female Negroes and food from houses".

(Letter from Lieutenant DE CAPRADO dated January 10th, 1726, National Archives, Col. C7A 10, p. 55, quoted in Jahlyssa SEKHMET, "L'histoire des Antilles françaises Guadeloupe Martinique - De la préhistoire à nos jours, (The history of the French West Indies Guadeloupe Martinique – From PreHistoric times to the present days) éd. Conscious education, 2018)

To tell the truth, slaveowners found it very difficult to maintain peace within the islands. In spite of frequent dispatches of soldiers to pacify the territory, Guadeloupe lived at the rhythm of multiple episodes of riots and revolts inevitably followed by their bloody repression (this was the case in 1656, of course, but also in 1710, 1730, 1748, 1752, 1802, etc.).

Yet, a great deal among us are unaware of this historical reality of the continuous resistance led by our enslaved African Ancestors. As a result, they continue to portray them as "slaves", enslaved and meek, having lost all sense of dignity, having adopted without any question, the Christian religion of their own executioners and waiting with hope the day when they will be set free. Thus, it is by borrowing these "ready-made thoughts" that completely falsify the reality of what our Ancestors were, that we have been gradually moving away from them and from what they had to transmit.

We were gradually losing the necessary sensitivity to feel that the country is still impregnated with all the things the Ancestors wanted to leave to us. Organized in nations (in plantations) or in black brotherhoods (in towns and cities), they were able to secretly recreate a social organization of their own, based on various forms of horizontal (among the living) and vertical (among generations) solidarity. This organization enabled everyone to share food, help the most vulnerable, save, transmit ancestral spiritual and cultural knowledge, and keep the community alive, despite the adversity of their condition and the fierceness of the amazing enterprise of mass destruction of their African identity in which they were going (through the assimilation and creolization process).

(See in particular : Luciani LANOIR-L'ÉTANG " Solidarity networks: In Guadeloupe yesterday and today ", ed. L'Harmattan, 2005)

It is true that, on closer inspection, the very definition of the word "slave" (a non-free person considered as an economic instrument that can be sold or bought, and under the dependence of a master) does not correspond in any way to the magnitude of the crime that was perpetrated on these African Ancestors. In fact, slaveholders were not satisfied to just deprive them of their freedom: they also wanted to *démouné* them (i.e. dehumanize them, as Philippe VERDOL put it in "Déshumanisation et surexploitation néocoloniales" (Neo Colonial dehumanization and overexploitation, ed. L'Harmattan, 2012).

Slaveowners made theories ..., even worse, they codified on the dehumanization of our Ancestors. They demanded from them the forgetting and absolute rejection of their African identity, their language, their culture, their history, their traditional know-how, their social organization, their traditional religions and spiritualities in order for them to completely immerse themselves in being good Creole Christians. This means, very concretely, that our Ancestors were forced to practice the religion that authorized, encouraged and justified the practice of the crime they were continuously suffering from. At that time, religion was mainly used as a means of pacifying our Ancestors by instilling in them the acceptance of their condition in expectation of a better future, and by impregnating them with values such as Christian forgiveness and submission to ecclesiastical authorities.

In fact, there is nothing neutral about using the word "slave" to name our Ancestors. The term conceals the magnitude and seriousness of the crime committed, as "slavery" is linked to the transatlantic slave trade, it can easily be assimilated to all forms of slavery known throughout ages. However, the main characteristic of slavery has always been the deprivation of liberty and of some civil rights (e.g. under ancient Rome). The crime committed against our

Ancestors was not limited to the mere deprivation of liberty, which is exactly what makes it so unique, because it went as far as the systemic and institutionalized negation of the human condition of other human beings (just because of the color of their skin).

By a process of nominalism, using the word "slave" to designate our enslaved African Ancestors allows us to minimize the crime committed and to hide in particular the whole historical reality of démounaj (dehumanization) and its psychosocial consequences undergone by several generations.

Incidentally, the choice of the word "slave" also makes it possible to create a docile and servile representation of our Ancestors, as the slave appears in our imagination as a defeated, tamed and weak person.

Institutions that thought up and carried out this crime against humanity (such as the French State or the community of families of settler slaves) have a vested interest in minimizing the reality of their crime, because today they are still there, still in control of the country, determined to get more and more out of it.

Indeed, the political project implemented by these institutions has been kept unchanged since their arrival in Guadeloupe in 1635. Indeed, for COLBERT, already in the 17th century, colonies had two assignments: to supply France with raw materials, rare and exotic foodstuffs, but also and above all to serve as outlets for products manufactured in France (*Encyclopaedia universalis, Volume 6, p. 77, 1990*).

Later on, following the second abolition of slavery in 1848, a colonial minister, Joseph ROMAIN-DESFOSSES, explained that, now that they had been emancipated, Africans had to abandon their "wild" customs to become true consumers in order to favor even more outlets for French products. (Josette FALLOPE, "*Esclaves et citoyens : les Noirs à la Guadeloupe au XIXe siècle dans les processus de résistance et d'intégration : 1802-1910*", *Société d'histoire de la Guadeloupe, (1992, p.364)* "*Slaves and citizens : Black People in Guadeloupe in the XIXth century in the process of resistance and integration : 1802-1910*" Society of the History of Guadeloupe, 1992, p. 364).

Today, even if Guadeloupe no longer plays the same role in terms of supplying raw materials, it remains largely in line with the political line set since the arrival of Europeans on this land: excessive exploitation of resources and people in the one hand, establishment and preservation of a structurally captive market in order to sell the famous "manufactured products" in an extremely lucrative way on the other hand.

All these political, strategic and symbolic issues are at stake behind the words, in particular the word "slave". Indeed, if descendants of enslaved Africans no longer make the link between France's political project during its slave-owning past and its current public policies, it is simply because, in the collective imagination, things have fundamentally changed since the abolition of slavery.

Slavery, just like the wage system, is for the perpetrators of the crime, a simple human resources management modality. The original political project is in no way called into question by the abolition of slavery. Admiral JAUREGUIBERRY, Minister of the Navy and Colonies in 1880 reminds us, not without a certain cynicism, that :

" (...) Slavery is abolished, our laws are proof of that. Officially, yes. In fact, no! (...). When the nations of Europe abolished the slave trade (officially) did they abolish slaves at the same time? The slaves stayed where they were, with their buyers. They simply changed their name: from captives in the trade, they became captives of a hut (...) ".

(Speech by the Minister of the Navy and Colonies, Admiral JAUREGUIBERRY, before the Senate 01/03/1880)

For this French State representative, despite the abolition of slavery, "slaves" remain symbolically "slaves". There is simply, a slight change in their status modalities. So, when descendants of enslaved Africans use the word "slave" to designate their ancestors, they give strength to this interpretation. At the same time, they move inexorably away from the powerful legacy left by the Ancestors.

Indeed, if there is one lesson to be learned from our history, it is that we are daughters and sons of survivors, everyday heroes, all survivors of an abominable crime.

We are alive today because each of our Ancestors, in his own way, knew how to resist by maintaining life, knew how to love and give life, knew how to transmit to those who succeeded him the love and respect of this life, so that from generation to generation, this life ultimately could reached us. It does not matter whether they were openly runaways or whether they resisted in the deadly context of the dwellings: our Ancestors, all of them as much as they were, managed to survive the unspeakable, to give life, to love and to transmit, so that we are today...

What is to be done now with what has been left for us? How to mobilize the immeasurable force that our Ancestors were able to generate to survive all this, while we apprehend them with words and values of their executioners?

It is for these reasons that the ICNP (International Committee of Black People) has launched a major campaign to call upon all the descendants of enslaved Africans (and more broadly all those who feel concerned), on the need to stop using the word "slave" to name our Ancestors.

We propose to name them AFRÈS (African reduced to slavery), but this is only our proposal. Everyone must find with his words the path leading to our Ancestors. The most important thing, for us, remains in that each one appropriates one's personal link with our Ancestors and that naturally understand that it can no longer be conceivable to treat our Ancestors with the same words and therefore the same paradigms as their executioners.

To rename our Ancestors with our own words, conceived with our own imagination cleared of borrowed and fallacious representations constitutes a true founding act of self-repair. Indeed, people feel strong and confident when anchored in their own self, when they are aware of the achievements and exploits of those who have forged their history, when they are able to mobilize all the power and strength coming from Ancestors by drawing on the heritage left and transmitted by them.

Now, as far as we are concerned, our ancestors' executioner imposed his culture, his values and his way of looking at ourselves, through assimilation and creolization. Through school, the Christian religion (Catholic and Protestant), mass media, the representations disseminated by official history, the apprehension we have facing the "savage" and the civilized, etc., we lose ourselves in conceiving ourselves through executioner's eyes, thinking that it is our own gaze, or worse, thinking that we merge with him, transcended that we are by a multi-speed universality. This is how we have been led, without realizing it, to treat our Ancestors like the same racists who tortured them, using their word "slave". All this only keep strengthening them and help intensify the prevailing negrophobia, and in fact, just contribute to weakening us.

In order to regain our strength and power, that cultivated by our Ancestors (notably through their ability to resist when no prospect of freedom seemed possible), we have no choice but to renew the heritage left by our Ancestors. Through the creative power of the verb, by naming our Ancestors (but also the political-psycho-social realities that permeate us) we can reweave this link by letting go of the executioner's reading grid to explore all that we really are. New horizons are opening up to us, because the fields of exploration are vast, whether artistic, spiritual, scientific (e.g. knowledge of plants), economic (e.g. our own savings and investment systems), political (e.g. systems of organisation of nations and black brotherhoods)...

This inevitably leads us to reposition ourselves in relation to our Ancestors, but also in relation to those who perpetrated the crime. Do we feel that we are sons of the blood of our Ancestors or creolized sons of the perpetrators of the crime suffered by our Ancestors?

The future will tell whether we will continue battles led by our Ancestors. They fought for our freedom... What will be our decision? Certainly, we have our own battles to fight to ensure a better tomorrow for our children. Will we do it by following and executing the project of those who have been leading us since the slave era (despite their crimes against our Ancestors) or will we do it by finding our own collective path in respect of the memory of our Ancestors?

Guadeloupe, 13/02/2020

Reparation, Recognition, Justice

By Her Majesty the Queen Mère Dòwòti Désir Hounon Houna II Guely

The AfroAtlantic Theologies & Treaties Institute

...Y bien, ahora os pregunto:

¿No tengo acaso... un abuelo nocturno

... un abuelo mandinga, conga, dahomeyano ?

¿Cómo se llama? ¡Oh, sí decídmelo !

¿ Andrés? ¿ Francisco ? ¿ Amable ?

¿ Cómo decís Andrés en Congo?

¿Cómo habéis dicho...

¿ El apellido, entonces !

--Nicolás Guillén, El apellido... elégia familiar,1958 (extract)

Many people believe that it is better to forget the past despite the fact that legal and cultural policies, commemorative landmarks such as monuments, generate a lot of interest within the diaspora concerned with African history. Although not expressed, the notion of spatial justice has a palpable impact on the innumerable manifestations requiring reparation both qualitatively and quantitatively. The argument put forward by Theo Van Boven, member of the International Commission of Jurists, is that the only valid response to brutal violations of human rights of victims are humanitarian principles. He points out that access to justice, as well as reparations for the harm done, are part of the corrective measures that societies must take. Van Boven is also among those who agree that there are four (4) main forms of reparations: restitution, compensation, rehabilitation, and guarantees that these facts will not happen again.

The ability of the State to find a righteous way to make wrongs right and to remedy injustices committed, so that dominant voices do not prevent minority voices from being heard, is the foundation of an egalitarian society. Ideally, civil rights of any society enable citizens to defend themselves by providing mechanisms for their common security, individual development and skills development. The political and social environment in which one evolves must be equipped with a legal infrastructure that promotes the construction and sustainable maintenance of these freedoms. A common vision on human rights laws would constitute the fundamental fabric of good governance and democracy worthy of the name, as it is accessible to all members of society, especially those who have been most deprived of them at the time when they needed to have their most inalienable rights respected.

Pluralism, lack of hegemony or diversity of populations, while being an asset for societies, are also sources of conflict. One of the virtues of democracy is to ensure the integration for all, despite frictions arising between different cultures, ethnicities or racial sensitivities. The uniformity of fundamental values is consolidated in the constitution of a State, electoral processes, the separation of powers and measures to protect against citizen rights violations. These societies policies must reflect these ideals if we are to live in a society without contradiction and inconsistency; however, the dignity of individuals must be preserved and ensured by the state. Cultural policies and practices of these societies must be pursued in tandem and integrated into a broad operational framework. However, we are witnessing a dynamic of great inertia that is casting a veil over cultural circles and attempts of societies to preserve their heritage, even though they pride themselves on their democratic institutions. In the manifestation of their public authorities, they are overwhelmed by State missions or civil society aspirations (certain sectors), for example, special interest groups. Jurists such as Van Hoven will have to consider to what extent the evolution of thinking - namely spatial thinking - may impact on societal values, dynamics of public authorities and reparation or restitution measures.

Every citizen has the right to know how the state has functioned through the historical relationships of its groups or the links with its government and other actors within common legal boundaries. Their asymmetrical landscape, be it political, economic, judicial, spatial or aesthetic, contributes to a permanent feeling among African descendants, given that there is no typically African formal recognition, knowledge or acceptance of traditional African values. This question addresses the issue of recognition both phenomenologically and legally, as well as ethically and otherwise, in view of the global dimension of "Afrophobia".

"I would feel much safer if I could be sure that I had an embassy where I could take refuge like a Korean does when things go wrong... We have no options, instead we are stuck in a place that does not recognize our history. I've heard prisoners and family members worried about their loved ones disappearing during administrative detention. Black people don't trust the government - we have never been trusted. Sydney K. retired police officer

The fear of disappearing into the hands of the state is not an irrational fear. Doudou Diène, serving at the United Nations as Special Rapporteur on Contemporary Forms of Racism, Racial Discrimination, Xenophobia and Related Intolerance (2002-2008), implored at the time to rethink the construction of reparations among Afro-descendants, emphasizing that silence and invisibility are the ideological pillars of permanent discrimination, exploitation and domination. Diène, argued in his 2006 article, Anti-Black Racism in the Era of Globalization: Issues, Challenges and Post-Durban Perspectives, in writing :

"Invisibility is economic and political. It dates back to the time of this construction (intellectual, historical and cultural) ... And was reinforced by the colonial enterprise".

But this invisibility is one of the profound consequences of anti-Black racism. It is all the more paradoxical since the Black, by virtue of his colour and all forms of manifestation of racism, is the one who is the most visible. The other dimension is silence. First of all, the historical silence, the fact that the history books that have been written, and that most European countries, have not only taken up in a more or less subtle way, have enfilmed, the intellectual construction of anti-Black racism, the burying of the Black in the image of a creature of pain.... A Homo doloris.

Diène's reflections on how the economic and political invisibility of Afro-descendants has an intellectual and cultural basis that parallels the historiography of silence. A point highlighted by Rolph Trouillot, "... the production of historical narratives involves an irregular contribution from competing groups and individuals who have unequal access to the means of such production... The supreme sign of power could be its invisibility, the supreme challenge, the exposure of its roots. Diène insists that the literature fails to mention that the African person creates the model of racism against Afro-descendants. In the end, we find ourselves engulfed in pain, homo doloris, a conclusion that is close to Diène's conclusion regarding reparations, a consideration that goes beyond the economic paradigm because it calls for the ethical, scientific, and educational aspects of reparations. His remarks focus on the political and literary, but the same could be said of commemorations. This subtle form of repression underscores the historical physical and mental inferiority of the environment in which Afrodescendants live.

This makes civil liberties all the more unstable. The absence speaks of segregation in the imagination, in histories, an absence of true conviviality even in the most multicultural and heterogeneous communities. We remember the dilemma of imprescriptibility. The Self cannot be erased, no matter how much time is given to destabilize the occurrence of a crime. In Mutombo Kanyana's essay: *"Recognition, Reparation and Reconciliation : from the Durban Conference to the current impasses. The Need for a New Paradigm" (2009), aptly summarizes the global reparations movement. It reminds us that, while the history of reparations began in the United States with the founders of the Pan-African Movement, we can pay particular attention to W.E.B. Dubois' 1947 text entitled "Petition in the Name of the Negroes". Others such as Paul Roberson, Malcolm X, Queen Mother Moore and Ray Jenkins continued this momentum, and it was not until the end of the 20th century that the creation of the Coordinating Committee for Reparations founded by Charles Ogletree served as a sounding board in the popular imagination of both whites and blacks. Reparation is a humanitarian response and a remedy to human rights violations. Bold and yet abortive efforts of civil society and government leaders such as Chief Bashorun Moshood K. O. Abiola (Nigeria, 1990) and President Jean Bertrand Aristide (Haiti, 2003) who have respectively provided significant financial support to this cause, is a well-documented legal and historical precedent for reparations, with consistent international media visibility, activist groups such as the US-based National Coalition of Blacks for Reparations (N'COBRA) Movement of December 12, and Ghanaian groups: the New African World*

Reparations and Reparation Truth Commission, and many others had concluded that $777 trillion was owed to black Africans and their descendants.

The World Conference against Racism, Racial Discrimination and other Forms of Intolerance held in 2001 in Durban, South Africa, which contracted the crushing weight of geo-historical, ethnic, gender-based and other crimes of colonialism, supported these efforts. At the United Nations Durban Review Conference on the Assessment of Racism, Racial Discrimination, Xenophobia and Related Intolerance held in Geneva, Durban Review, the coalition was successfully supported, as issues related to reparations were overwhelmed by US demands to change the terms of the outcome document. The United States continued by systematically boycotting the process, including the absence of the Black Council Congress. As recently as June 2009, the day before Juneteenth (the day before the emancipation of slaves in 1865 was honoured), the US Senate passed a resolution apologizing for slavery and including a disclaimer. A non-binding resolution (and it is important to emphasize that it is non-binding) stating that the Government of the United States of America "... recognizes the fundamental injustices, cruelty, brutality, and inhumanity of slavery, and the Jim Crow laws, and apologizes to African Americans on behalf of the people of the United States for the harm done to them and their ancestors who suffered under the Jim Crow laws. The apology, it should be noted, was issued under the administration of President Barack Hussein Obama, the first president of African descent.

Although his efforts have not yet borne fruit since 1989, U.S. Representative John Conyers, Jr. (b. 1929) persists in introducing H. R. 40 to Congress : "*To recognize the fundamental injustice, cruelty, brutality, and inhumanity of slavery within the United States and the 13 American colonies between 1619 and 1865, and to establish a commission to examine the institution of slavery, and thereafter de jure and de facto, and the economic discrimination against African Americans, its impact on African Americans, to make recommendations to Congress on appropriate means to remedy it, and for other purposes.*" The 1999 Act (similar to the 1989 H.R. 1745) was named H.R. 40 as a symbol of the "40 acres and a mule" promise that was made to African slaves during the civil war and never kept. The 7-member commission is due to return to Congress with a series of recommendations.

In 2001 the International Movement for Reparations / Konvwa Pou Réparasyon, in collaboration with the worldwide movement for reparations, started a boat from the coast of Senegal to Martinique. Every year a ship convoy for reparation makes a tour of the island of Martinique. The march also recognizes the enormous efforts of abolitionists in Guadeloupe and France, including Louis Delgrès (1766-1802) and Victor Schöelcher (1804-1893). Since then, in anticipation of the march, two people's courts have concluded that slavery and colonization were crimes against humanity (2009, 2011). Currently a civil lawsuit for reparations is being filed in France. In 2012, on the other hand, reparations objectives were highlighted including obtaining funds for the creation of a genealogical research institute for all descendants of Africans; a compensation fund for Haiti; a meeting aimed at creating an organization of international jurists focused on financial reparations; with protection for human rights defenders/lawyers. In 2017-2018 the French courts of justice rejected the request for reparations on the grounds that crimes against humanity had exceeded the statute of limitations. MIR's legal team has appealed and expects a response in 2020 from these courts.

(3) In 2013, member states of the Caribbean Common Market (CARICOM) finally gave in to civil society urging them to jointly submit a claim for reparations with the CARICOM 10-Point Plan for the Justice Program, through a Committee for Reparations led by Sir Hillary Beckles who then spoke before the British Parliament in 2014. After highlighting the genocidal impact of slavery in the Caribbean and the damage it has done to the fabric of society to this day, he made an urgent appeal for justice for reparations through health, education and human resource initiatives, as well as various development issues to be considered as a legal, moral issue that British diplomatic officials around the world need to take into account. In 2019 Britain has agreed to pay £20 million in compensation.

The State runs the risk of diminishing its capacity by not recognizing the extent of its human capital. The development of every human being is psychological, moral, ethical, intellectual, spiritual, material and spatial. Human rights are intrinsically linked to human development and our memory respectfully reminds us of this reality. Denying memory leads to the loss of human achievements. It provides one group with a sense of moral superiority and imbues others with inferiority complexes. Refusal to acknowledge the epic nature of this tragedy means that no meaningful apology is possible, and without such an apology, no reconciliation is possible. Without reconciliation, injustices cannot be properly redressed. As long as injustices persist in a society, antagonism, non-conviviality, disparities and inequalities will continue to prevail.

Guillen's final request in El appellido... elegia familiar asks the monumental, pointed and most fundamental human question that virtually all Africans in the Diaspora are asking themselves on the verge of being disconnected (especially those who have been ignorant of their origins for a number of generations): Sabéis mi otro appellido... el appellido sangriento y capturado... Que paso entre cadenas sobre el mar? Basically... "*Do you know my other name? The last one, bloody and captured... Who crossed the sea in chains?...*" His play tells us that our shared narratives are incomplete because mnemonic, social and linguistic historical references have been omitted. He seeks one of three thematic pillars of the Decade 2015-2024 for African Descendant Peoples, "Recognition, Justice, Development".

This recognition has a restorative justice function and suggests that there is an ability to recognize the distinct nature, required value or perceived value of a person, object or place. The relationship between recognition and identity is also influenced by memory. Legally, recognition is attached to one's role in society. It refers to its representation in the state and also concerns the ability to shape its outcomes. Recognition also includes interacting with the factors that amplify its representation within the state, including the capacity to improve it in order to form more equitable spaces of existence, to reduce and eliminate disparities that contribute to producing injustice and hinder development. The construction of memorials should help to build broader strategies for reparations, particularly where scholars such as Kanyana and Diène have advocated a broader definition that includes ethical, economic, scientific and academic components beyond the financial demands of civil society. As a mnemonic device, reparations promote a broader, fractal and sophisticated interpretation of the political landscape and its historical context. Recalling memory and recognition is linked to the dynamics of our governments, and a sustained presence on all fronts is necessary to achieve restitution, especially for those considered minorities in their societies. Memorials encourage the visibility and preservation of history. It allows us to acknowledge evidence of the human dimension of others in the landscape through their historical presence, origins and place. Tout moun, se moun, everyone has a story.

REPARATIONS —An an urgent requirement for humanity

FINAL NOTES

1.   Legal scholar Theo Van Boven has written extensively on the right to reparations for victims of various international human rights violations, providing principles and guidelines for the United Nations and other global institutions to follow.

2.   Late Moshood Abiola made a significant financial contribution to the reparation movement in 1990. After running for the presidency of Nigeria, he was imprisoned for political activism. A few days after his release, Abiola died in mysterious circumstances (1998). President Aristide was personally discredited by the media and the U.S. government, provoking a coup d'état in 1991 that ended Haiti's first democratically elected head of state. He returned to power in 2003 only to see his challenges to legitimate power coincide with his demands for reparations to the French government equivalent to the $21 billion that the French government illegally stripped from the young nation-state just after independence.

3.   In 2013, the CARICOM Heads of Government issued a request for redress addressed to the Governments of the United Kingdom, the Netherlands, France and others. The decision was aligned with efforts of European Union Members of Parliament under the leadership of Jean Jacob Bicep, among others, to set an official date for the recognition of slavery and European colonization, recommending the establishment of a regional commission for reparations based in the Caribbean. In September 2013,

his first conference for reparations was held in the island-states of Saint Vincent and the Grenades, under the auspices of Prime Minister Ralph E. Gonsalves. Key determinations include:

a.   All CARICOM countries form their own National Reparations Commissions.

b.   All CARICOM Regional Commissions will be formed at the meeting of National Commissions in September 2013.

c.   The University of the West Indies (English West Indies) is requested to establish a Reparations Research Unit to provide working guidelines to the CARICOM Commission, a request made by the CARICOM leadership.

This action has accompanied a large number of recommendations made by African descendants to achieve their goals of *"Recognition, Development of Justice. The request submitted to the United Nations General Assembly was entitled"* Report of the Working Group of Experts in the Field of African Descendant Peoples, 11th Session, Addendum to the Draft Programme of Action for the Decade for African Descendant Peoples. "Agenda of the 21st session of the Human Rights Council, Article 9, 3 August 2012. The statements are consistent with the letter of 29 July from Abdurahhman M. Shalgam, Ambassador and Permanent Representative of Libya, which highlighted the need for compensation for damages caused by colonialism, proposed to the United Nations. Furthermore, in the recommendations made at AfricaRat-Berlin in 2010, the People's Tribunal concluded that colonization is a crime against humanity at the 125th commemoration of the Berlin-

Congo Conference (1885). Although not discussed during the conference, the environment, whether natural or man-made, must be taken into account as a reference for memory, and in this approach the inventory of all relevant sites must accompany it.

4.   Presentation by Stephen Campbell, New UNESCO Approaches to Interpreting Slavery in Sites and Museums, University of Virginia, February 2018.

This text is an edited chapter from, Wòch kase wòch: Redlining a Holocaust, Memorials and the People of the AfroAtlantic published by Gran Bwa Press, New York, under the author's name: Dòwòti Désir2020.

The deconstruction of the Kamite couple as a sequel to the destruction of the Kamite family by transatlantic slavery. What reparations for so many daily crimes gone unpunished?

By Juliette Sméralda

Sociologist, writer, researcher

The Kamite woman in the social and sexual hierarchical order of slavery societies of the 'New World' undergoes, on a daily basis, humiliation, sexual exploitation, rape, physical violence, punishment, infantilization and inferiorization, coarseness, symbolic violence, degrading treatment, etc.. The vocabulary used against her is most often scatological or sexual, systematically scornful. However, these bestializing metaphors, symbolic of the inhuman treatment she was undergoing, have not succeeded in destroying her.

The Kamite woman

Transatlantic slavery in the Americas in the 17th-19th centuries brought together populations from civilizations that had nothing in common. It was "*above all a system designed to extract maximum profit from a people of restive subjects who were forced (Gerda Lerner, 1972:19)[53]. The inhumanity of their living conditions was that they were prisoners of a deeply racist and tyrannical system that insisted on seeing them as inferior beings; a sub-humanity deprived of the most elementary legal rights, at the mercy of the arbitrary actions of European and American settlers, planters, masters and managers of slave societies, who reduced them not only to the function of child bearing[54], but also to that of producers, mistresses, consumers, educators...*

Between their reification as sexual, reproductive objects - bellies rather than women and mothers - exotic objects, the Western and colonial imaginary has applied itself to constructing Kamite women as stigmatic figures (in the negative representations attached to their hyper sexualized bodies and their systematically degraded social status). So much so that they inherited a reputation of libertinage that blurred them from the monstrous exploitation to which they were subjected in the slavery economic system ...

Few sources document the social and cultural history of

---

[53] *From slavery to segregation, Black women in White America,* Denoël/Gonthier.

[54] « in the slaveholders eyes, kamite women were not really seen as mothers, but rather as mere reproductive objects for keeping the labour force in balance. Just considered as bellies, or cattle which value was estimated in the light of their reproductive capacity » (Angela Davis, 1981).

Kamite women's slavery. Too scattered or too rare are those that bear witness to their daily and intimate life. Where they exist, these sources are so manipulated that they must be referred to with caution. "We have been believing for a long time," wrote Y. Knibiehler & R. Goutaltier (1985:9)[55] , "It was long believed (that these women) had no history... It is now well known that even if they were only subjected to events and laws..., they did have a history of their own, which... also weighs on that of men. "

Generally speaking, writes Gerda Lerner (p. 25), "the life of female slaves was in every way more arduous, more difficult, and even more limited than that of men. They had as much work to do as men. They were given even the hardest work (Angela Davis 1981)[56], which is now referred to as " men's work. While they were subject to the same duties as men, pregnancy and child rearing were additional burdens that greatly increased their overwork. They were punished brutally, whether they were pregnant or infirm. Their love for their children was deliberately used to chain them to their masters and to the plantation. Children could be used as hostages any time if they tried to escape. Therefore, they were less likely to escape than men.

---

[55] *The woman during the time of colonies*, Stock.

[56] *Women, race and class, Women*, 1981.

The appropriation of the body and sexuality of the Kamite woman

In the plantation, physical use was the core of the settler's relationship with his "property". "Physical use expressed in its smallest, most succinct form: sexual use. The only possible physical use" - "use of a woman's body" - "when the encounter is fortuitous and when there are no stable social ties". "(C. Guillaumin, 1992:23)[57]. The form of appropriation to which she is subjected is non-monetary, since if the black woman is treated as a prostitute, her condition as a slave requires neither her consent, nor financial compensation, nor monetary time. Rape[58] constitutes a violent and abusive appropriation of her body, since the woman does not generally lend herself to this form of appropriation of her being. "This situation ... killed her psychologically ... annihilated all self-respect". She felt... (deeply) dirty, disrespected, despicable, vile. "And it went very, very far into her soul. And this suffering has continued since that time in the West Indian woman[59]. "

---

[57] *Sex, race and the practice of power / L'idée de nature*, Editions Côté-femmes

[58] Role of rape - appropriation of women sexuality - in these fantasies (sexual intercourse without counterpart) : « service » ripped away by force...

[59] Maryse Laclef-Feldman, « West Indian matrifocality : its evolution », International Victimology diary, JIDV Victimology and Psychological Trauma review from 2002 - ISSN 1925-721X.

The Kamite man

The Kamite man was stripped of all attributes related to the power that his civilization had endowed him with, before he was deported to the Americas and reduced to a state of slavery. During the time of his enslavement, colonists and their societies worked together to emasculate him, to remove any spirit of competition and any desire to compete with the whites[60]. Reduced to the most degrading state of a stallion, exploited in its most basic function as a "breeding animal", he was never placed in a position to exercise any functions of husband and father, much less to have family responsibilities, during centuries of slavery and colonial domination. In the absence of institutions, customs on which the unity of the Kamite family should have been based were in ruins, seriously damaged (Laclef-Feldman, 2002). Thus, this family had no choice but to adapt to the colonial disaster by founding homes that were places of violent conflict (idem).

As a result of tragedies that have plagued him for centuries, the enslaved Kamite man "underwent a painful journey through historical stages of an enslavement that enslaved him, frustrated and alienated him through shameful acts and perpetual abuses against himself. "In all his suffering,

---

[60] Since the slavery times, the Black man has been dispossessed of all forms of power, his authority and parenthood that had been captured by the master ...

221

therefore, he was unable to take on the life of a couple. He continued to flee in irresponsibility, to flee in lightness, to flee in adultery, to flee in aggressiveness towards women. His authority has been so abused (...) that there is violence in him, from time to time. ".

Constantly confronted with destructive scenarios and exposed to the material and moral violence of her man, the Kamite woman in the Americas will more or less succeed in consolidating her material situation, but the Kamite man, who has not founded social institutions in which he lives, will only accidentally be a security for the Kamite woman and child....

The kamite child

When he was born; when he had not been removed from slavery misfortunes by infanticide, the Kamite child belonged first to slavers, just such as was the case for his parents. "The practice of mistresses buying young children for themselves as little handymen fuelled the custom of separating children from their parents (Gerda Lerner, 1972). "Parents are almost never consulted when it came to deciding what would happen to their children; they have as little control over them as pets have over their youngs. This indifference violates all natural and social feelings, all tenderness; slaves are treated as if they were deprived of all human emotion. "(Lerner, p. 31).

Here are echoes of some of the dramas experienced daily by parents who are powerless to protect their children:

"One day Fennel came home from the fields and his daughter was gone. His wife was on the ground, passed out. Their baby had been sold. [61]"

The law of utter arbitrariness reigned, as this text from *Roots* (p. 257) shows: "(...) Black babies still in their mothers' wombs were given as gifts, offered as stakes in card games or cockfights. Le Violoneux had told him the story of this master who, on his deathbed, had bequeathed in his will to each of his five daughters one of the unborn babies of his slave Mary, aged fifteen - and already fat. Black children were given as collateral for loans, babies still in the womb were claimed by creditors, paid for by debtors to get out of a debt. He knew that during slave auctions in the county capital, a sturdy six-month-old black infant - the age at which he could be presumed to survive – reached the price two hundred dollars."

"A planter from Baton Rouge... bought Randall. Throughout the transaction, Eliza screamed loudly... she begged the man not to buy her son without buying her and her little Emily... Freeman turned wildly to her, raised the whip in his

---

[61] *La Virginienne,(the Virginian woman)*, Barbara Chase Riboud, Albin Michel, 1981.

hand and ordered her to stop the noise if she didn't want to be whipped. He was not going to tolerate such conduct - such whining - and if she did not stop at once he would take her into the yard to give her a hundred lashes.... She continued to beg and implore in the most pitiful way in the world that they should not be separated... But nothing helped... the deal was struck and Randall had to go alone".

" No attention from most inhabitants to the animal education of their slaves' children. Mothers carried them on their shoulders to the fields and left them abandoned all day long, in the heat of the burning sun. I conclude from all these vices that these are the main causes of the small population of Negroes in our colonies, and it is an almost general evil in all our Negro colonies.[62] "

The Kamite family

Transatlantic slavery was that long period of unparalleled violence, of destruction of the Person, of Humanity and of the Kamite family; marked by the sale of mothers, fathers and children torn away from their parents.

The persistent suffering endured by slaves exposed to cruel

---

[62] Le marquis de Fénelon, governor of Martinique, 11th avril 1764 letter sent to the minister, quoted by par G. Debien (2000:362-363).

separations that destroyed every emotional ties between them has unfortunately not been well studied. Gerda Lerner reports that even when married, chambermaids and seamstresses often slept in their mistress' apartments on the floor. One of them had been married for eleven years, but had never been allowed to sleep anywhere but in her mistress' room. Domestic slaves were rarely allowed to socialize with each other during the day, since their work kept them apart. Cases were not uncommon where husband and wife did not belong to the same owner.

"The West Indian family has adapted to the colonial disaster", but relations within the Kamite couple are particularly fraught with suffering (Laclef-Feldman).

(Laclef-Feldman). "Since black women were not "women" by standard, the slave system discouraged phallocracy among black men. Husbands and wives, fathers and daughters were all placed under the absolute guardianship of their masters. Favouring phallocracy would have been a dangerous threat to power. Moreover, since black (women) were not considered to be representatives of the "weaker sex" or "mistress of houses", black men could not claim the title of "head of the family" or even provide for their material needs. (...) Men, women and children "maintained" class(es) of slaver(s). They all worked, side by side in plantations, according to an undifferentiated pattern that did not structure any hierarchy between different members of the family...". (A. Davis, 1981:17).

In (post-)-colonial society, the pseudo institution that matrifocality becomes in its colonial and racist version, built on the evacuation of the father, weakens women. Europeans, who considered the reproduction of Africans in the Americas as a pure breeding problem, only intended it to promote the growth of their "demographic capital". They therefore forbade slaves to be married. The man was "resigned" from the family and transformed into a sexual performer, an irresponsible sire. Maryse Laclef-Feldman analyses it in terms of pathology, resulting "from the history of triangular slavery, which led to the destruction of the father's role, and the need for the mother's preponderant influence in the education of children, It is in this deleterious climate that a systematic acculturation of (Kamites) to European values and norms was instituted when, in the 19th century, a minimum of integration became necessary to continue colonial exploitation. "

Applying the white couple paradigm to black women excluded them from anything positively defined and socially recognized. This exclusion was responsible for the emergence of colonial myths designed to water down the sociological disasters caused among Kamites by the ruinous state in which the slave and colonial systems left them and their families when they were any left.

The invention of the "male-female" is significant of the effects of such disasters transformed into the founding myth of the colonial destruction of the Kamite family reduced to single parenthood, in a world of Western values, where male domination and white supremacy are expressed in all their extent .

The colonial construction of the male-female only maintains by default a link with the Kamite idea that the woman was **"the ridge beam of the house"**, which assured her a great independence based on the respect of her personality, her lineage, and her spouse. She was an economic force, occupying an important place. She did not exist solely through her status as a wife or a submissive woman.

She occupied, more often than not, an honourable place in the life of the community, in the direction of affairs concerning her people[63].

The very high rate of social failure among the Kamites of the Americas is not unrelated to the destruction of the historical ties that structured their human community through a whole network of intra-familial and social ties that were all the more effective because so complex. In these societies that

---

[63] Sarah Kala-Lobé, « Situation of women in the traditional society), dans *La civilisation de la femme dans la tradition africaine*, (the civilization of women in the African tradition) Colloque d'Abidjan, 3-8 juillet 1972, Présence Africaine, 1975, [92-105].

practiced socioracial discrimination as an ethic, Kamite youths, nearly 50% of whom grow up in matriarchal homes, are disinherited because they lack a family bulwark. Faced with having to assume alone the duties of two parents, the mother is quickly overwhelmed and children are left to their own devices, psychotropic drugs and delinquency (Laclef-Feldman, 2002).

Despite countless abuses inflicted on them by the inhuman system of slavery, and the disastrous role that it made them play against the men in their community, we must consider, like Gerda Lerner, that Kamite women "participated much more in all aspects of the resistance than historians have recognized so far; from rebellion to sabotage and passive resistance."Their efforts must be taken into account when we think of the struggle that blacks waged ... to survive. "

French Guiana: Knowing about crime against humanity so as not to perpetuate it

By Apa Mumia Makeba (Benoît Bechet)

President of MIR Guyana

It is in the rejection of the other that awareness begins and our Ancestors have experienced this in their flesh since they were torn from their native soil.

When this manifestation is prolonged through so-called progressives, the rupture becomes inevitable. This is how in 1967 the largest trade union centre in French Guiana cut the umbilical cord that linked it to the CGT. In its statutes, the demand for the national independence of French Guiana was enshrined.

These few words explain the place and context in which the notion of crime against humanity and reparations emerged.

Nearly ten years after the death of the founder and first secretary of the UTG, Turenne Radamonthe, everyone had every reason to justify their disengagement from the decree to commemorate the abolition of slavery. However, the commemorative events received a great deal of media coverage. By remaining silent we became an accomplice in a situation that was betraying the memory of our trade union line as well as the history of the resistance and even worse, it gave pride of place to those promoting the cult of *the great White saviour.*

It was when the founder of the UTG on June 9, 1989, that the central decided, one year later to mark the event that would finally be called *June 9 & 10, Days of Resistance against capitalist and colonialist exploitation*. All demonstrations have since then, been associated with basic components of the people of Guyana, namely the Guyanese of the Maroni Valley and the coast and those whom settlers have always referred to as Amerindians. These components form a community of suffering, but also of resistance.

In the year of the centenary of this decree, the "Sa ou pa konèt gran pasé ou" committee, including the UTG, developed the subject from the angle of crime against humanity, denounced the falsification of history and this, during a major conference held in February 1998 by Professor Obenga. The latter demonstrated the basis of the crime and dismantled the academic untruths stemming from the ethnological sciences devoted to Africa and based on theories of the philosopher Hegel. That same year the regional council of Guyana had to make a decision on the proposal of the elected representatives of the M.D.E.S. Although the assembly, which was represented by a majority of people of African descent, and despite the success of this conference affirming that this tragedy was a crime against humanity, the majority group of this assembly subordinated its decision to other "investigations" in order to have a more "enlightened" opinion.

It was only following the mobilization of Afro-descendants in Durban in 2001, the law recognizing slavery as a crime against humanity - promoted by Christiane Taubira and the publication of Rosa Amelia Plumelle Urible's book "White

Ferocity"- that the question of reparations took shape through the creation of the M.I.R. atè Gwiyàn.

During a conference held on 10 June 2003, which had the value of a people's congress, in the presence of the same regional president, it was decided to build a place of remembrance, against the tide of official history, and it was in the commune of Rémire, the first place of deportation of Africans, but also of resistants and runaways, it was decided to install the place of remembrance there.

On June 10th 2004, in French Guiana, the first convoy for repairs (Konvwa Pou Reparasyon) began, with the laying of the foundation stone by the M.I.R. (including several trade union, associative and political components and delegations from Martinique and Guadeloupe). On June 10th 2008, the erection of the Statue of Runaways for Freedom, which was the first monument paying tribute to African Ancestors struggle against the Maafa*. In 2009, the official inauguration with Afro-American Indian rituals, later on International Women's Day, the change of name of the place housing the "Statue of Runaways for Freedom" to that of the heroine Adelaide Tablon. Some historians and history professors criticized this choice of name, arguing that her history was not part of the period before abolition. This is forgetting that the crime has not yet stopped, that it is still going on, as Hegel's thesis based on geographical determinism and arguing that Africa being a hot zone could not be conducive to reason. More recently, Sarkozy's speech in Dakar and numerous examples demonstrate that racism is the ideology and substance of the African tragedy.

In the case of our mother Adélaïde Tablon, she was fighting against this sort of racism; moreover, she is a strong symbol, because she won the fight that opposed her to colonial authorities who wanted to impose a colonist in place of a duly elected representative from African descent in the Roura district.

The struggle for reparations finds its limits in the lack of knowledge of the crime, and therefore in a poor assessment of the harm done. This does not make it possible to identify victims or perpetrators. Yet, the occupation of French Guiana by a State exercising its power outside its territorial borders seems obvious. Unless one validates the idea that Melanesian-Africans are sub-human, as they are the ones who have always been excluded from almost all areas of public, social, economic and other life.

However, reparations cannot be merely symbolic, unless they disregard themselves, and there again it would be to internalize the inferiority of people of African descent.

What is our **geopolitical** reality today when countries around us, Surinam, Brazil, Guyana, Venezuela forming the Guyana Plateau, are independent and that few bilateral and economic cooperation agreements between Guyana (under French trusteeship) and its neighbours only exist by proxy.

The **cultural** reality should allow traditional practices to survive before the Maafa*, but political domination is so strong that communities that resisted yesterday are won over by foreign values, and when they do not fall into the assimilationist policy that affects a very large part of the inhabitants of the Guyanese coastline, many of its members, in the interior of the country, commit suicide.

In terms of worship, on the vast majority of the coastline and now on the banks of the Maroni River, there is a spread of imported religions under the colonial regime.

In the **educational system**, all establishments taken together (including universities), teaching is part of a European civilizational project. The curricula and the yearly school calendar respect the French vision in all its aspects, including when they are in contradiction to climatic and seasonal realities.

The aerospace industry dominates **economic activity** to the detriment of agriculture and animal husbandry. France has achieved its objective by expropriating farmers and growers from their family, social and economic base by settling between Kourou and Sinnamary, a region formerly known for its food self-sufficiency. This region had demonstrated that even during the 39-46 war in Europe, its population not only did not have food problems experienced by the capital city, but even supplied it with livestock. Today, French Guiana is dependent on an economic activity that is subservient to the satellite market. Space activity has not come to supplement existing activities, but to replace them. Today, economic activity has become dependent on subsidies. The colonial symbol of French Guiana is space, which directly serves interests of France and Europe. It benefits from very strong protection by the State to the extent that, until today, no medical authority has looked into the health impact of space activity. Fortunately, there was the great general strike of October 92, bringing together the four major trade unions UTG, CDTG, FO and FEN under the name M.S.U. (Mouvement Syndical Unifié) which denounced this dependence on space at the end of major works in Kourou in favour of the development of space activity.

In 2017 this was still the case with the lighting union UTG before being joined by collectives, the starting point of the March/April 2017 movement.

From a linguistic point of view, the linguistic variants of languages spoken in Guyana by people of African descent have an African root and syntax, although denied by the colonial administration. These languages are not in danger of disappearing as languages, but over time they are losing their African substratum and this is the objective.

A quotation from Aimé Césaire 1962 on the so-called Creole language quoted on page 9 of the book Jean Luc Divialle indicates the point: "I am not at all 'creolizing', and this for several reasons. Perhaps I have a very strong feeling of the infirmity of this language called "Creole" which really seems to me a small regional language of extremely limited scope. Not at all that I despise it, but in order to make it a valid instrument, it would have been necessary to make an effort on this language as prodigious as that made by men of the Pléiade, where men of the 1st century made out of the French language so that it would be a valid and usable instrument". Here is another perspective that cannot be done by proxy and which falls into the field of reparation: to revive our language that violence has not spared.

Finally, fundamentally, if reparations are a matter of justice, this issue is obviously eminently political and it is within this context that a law was passed by French parliamentarians, but the reparation component was cut out, in order to make it normative. It is up to people to make it functional through mobilization. However, the politico-administrative situation in countries under French rule remains very embarrassing and France has decided to wage war against communitarianism. It does not specify that this war is targeted against a particular community, because there are communities in France which have their own schools, their own banks, their places of worship, etc., and which are not threatened.

As a result, the issue of the consubstantiality of reparations and French Guiana's access to full sovereignty remain the most appropriate watchword today.

The situation of Caribbean States confirms this conclusion with the progress made on the issue of reparations.

Self-repair allows us to enlighten, but above all to become aware of our ability to live with dignity outside the system of predation imposed and accepted by all, in every area.

The Caribbean body: how can art repair the organic memory of historical suffering?

By Patricia Donatien

University Professor

University of West Indies

A Man cannot be understood, if he is not considered and accepted in his totality and singularly in his relationship to himself, in his relationship to his body, and in the sensual link maintained by him with the universe, notably through his spiritual and artistic activities.

In the Caribbean space, marked by the violence of history and systems, the individual dispossessed of the free enjoyment of his body has for centuries repressed his true feelings, going so far as to develop a virulent syndrome well known in popular medicine: wheat, an internal wound, a sense disorder and a psychosomatic trace of the physical and mental suffering endured for centuries. The Caribbean man, in his bodily relationship to the world and contrary to the stereotypical image spread by colonial and exotic thinking, is a dark being marked by the brutality and corruption of history. Thus, for many Caribbean, the relationship to the body remains problematic, as it is marked by a popular, institutional or commercial discourse in which exotic, sexualized, devaluing language prevails. This is conducive to racist fantasies and ideologies that constitute psychological and symbolic violence, as well as the perpetuation of self-rejection and social and racial divisions inherited from the plantation pigmentocracy.

For decades, some precursors have been strongly denouncing the imposture and falsity of preconceived discourses on the Caribbean body, whose true language and messages carry fragmentation and memory pain. Contemporary Caribbean artists: writers, painters, sculptors and choreographers approach the body and the sense language from the angle of a deepening opposed to exotic visions, revealing in a sometimes brutal approach, the violence and ugliness of marks coming from the past and traumas of the present that try to hide under the mask of the exaltation of the body: hypersexual body, often disproportionate and valued in all its excesses.

How to manage then, so that this body still stigmatized, rejected (colour of skin and hair which are still perceived and received as social barriers) or enclosed in restrictive and belittling prejudices , can be repaired and ceases to be in particular for Martinican Afro-descendants, a source of suffering and a social, economic and personal obstacle. One of possible paths alongside what psychoanalysis and ontological reparation resulting from a revision of language can offer (notably the abandonment of animal terminologies due to Moreau de St Méry's[64] classifications) is art and what literature, dance, visual arts can offer to beings in a reparative revision of themselves.

In order to attempt to provide an answer to this problem, it is necessary first to explore the meaning of the body in the postcolonial societies in which we live; firstly through the study of the image of an excessively denatured self that has been overused by advertising, social networks, websites and other media, and secondly through the vision of the body given by contemporary Caribbean artistic expressions that show *le language de la blès*, a raw body language of non-avoidance and counter-exoticism that codifies and structures recent works. Through this true aesthetic of bodies and senses confronted with pain and excess, we will attempt to demonstrate how, in a reconstruction of his spatial body and in a guilt-free and renewed projection of his sensual perceptions, today's Caribbean artist reconstructs history, space and tells his world and can also to some extent help the one who suffers in his body to reconcile with himself. To get there, we will see how the relationship to the body in the Caribbean revolves around a memory and an experience of the body.

---

[64] Topographic, physical, civilian, political and historical description of the french side of Saint-Domingue island. 1798. Moreau de St Méry declares through a supposedly scientifically- based ideology a classification system for Black people according to the amount of "white" or "black" blood they have within their body. He goes as far as declaring that there are 9 categories combining around 128 possible "genetic cross".

What is a body, what is the memory of the body for the Caribbean man?

Frantz Fanon says he doesn't want to be a slave to slavery. This implies for me that one cannot simply ignore the historical phenomenon of slavery; that one must not be impulsively subjected to its persistent trauma. Overcoming is projective exploration. The slave is first of all the one who does not know. The slave of slavery is the one who does not want to know.   (Glissant The Caribbean Discourse 129)

For many of us Caribbean, historical traumas of slavery and colonization seem so remote and impertinent that they no longer "constitute a plausible version of effects of destruction developing between generations; however, research and an increasingly enlightened understanding of our history have enabled many others to understand that colonization and slavery as historical phenomena, as well as the anthropological characteristics of Creole societies, are at the very root of the violence that people still suffer from, nowadays. However, it is more difficult for us to discern how these historical phenomena are embedded in our intimacy, in our understanding of ourselves, in our relationship to our bodies and to the other's relationship to those bodies. It is often only art, in the midst of socio-historical confusion, that cries out our truth to us. Michela Marzano, a researcher at the CNRS (French National Centre for Scientific Research) tells us that: "Our body is one of the evidences of our existence: it is in and with our body that we are born, that we live, that we die, it is in and with our body that we build our relationships with others... our body is an object".

The problem in our stigma-bearing societies is that seeing the body as an object is not just a philosophical postulate, but a reality that our great-grandparents experienced in all the ignominy of the denial of humanity. Through the collective unconscious, through cognitive charges, through the transmission of habitus, but also through a symbolic violence that submits us and makes us agents of this imposed violence, we have kept this understanding and definition of our bodies as objects buried within us. For our bodies are memory bodies.

Indeed, slavery and colonization were eras of denial of humanity during which human beings were reduced to furniture, deported, sold, exploited and tortured. Bodies that have become objects, reified as Aimé Césaire tells us, are denied in their relationship to the spirit, to the soul, to become animal entities or even producing machines, to such an extent that in the Creole language, the body is independent and acts against us, as an agent of suffering:

Kó mwen ka fè mwen mal,

Pié mwen ka brilè mwen, janb mwen ka lansé mwen

Thus, the Caribbean and especially the Martinican does not

say "I suffer", he expresses the idea of an independent body that would not belong to him and that would impose suffering on him; the body in its whole and parts that make it up carry wounds and torment us. These wounds in question are both wounds of personal memory, sometimes imprinted in the flesh by the loss of a loved one, by an accident, by an illness, and wounds of collective memory, inflicted by the violence of history and in the perpetually flouted sense of freedom and justice. In this regard, Paul Ricoeur tells us, we must recall the paradox of memory, which is that there is nothing more personal, more intimate and more secret than memory, but that one another's memories, between relatives, neighbours, strangers, refugees - and also adversaries and enemies - are incredibly intertwined, sometimes to the point that we no longer distinguish in our stories what belongs to each of us: wounds of memory are both solitary and shared.

Thus, in the reception we have of our bodies, especially when they are suffering, vestiges of work activities and sufferings of the past are present, but they are also impacted by a number of very devaluing perceptions that are not unrelated to colonial philosophies and that maintain the idea, still present in a great many minds, that Negroid characteristics are vectors of ugliness, of inferiority.

Indeed, Caribbean populations have violently encoded the perception inflicted on them by dehumanizing systems of slavery and colonization; a perception perpetuated by agents of violence that are religious, administrative and educational institutions. Caribbean marked in their DNA by this devaluation, this rejection of self, this *blés* were thus forced to consider their bodies as distant objects with which they sometimes maintain traumatic links; and this painful tension is still a reality for many today.

The thinking and body perception that Art may allow

Faced with difficulties mentioned and the reality of an almost pathological relationship that the Caribbean, and particularly the Martinican, maintain with their bodies, how can art intervene as a regulator and perhaps a reversal power of representations of the self? In traditional societies, not determined by the power of technique, it is the symbolic order that predominates in which the relationship between the body and the social is closely intertwined with nature and mythical figures; but present-day societies tend to obliterate the symbolic function of the body.

It is undoubtedly in this flaw that art can interfere and find, perhaps, a place of mediator, a restorative function, in the sense that art possesses this power to link the symbolic to the real and everything that is of the order of the psychic, of the imaginary to the rational functioning of the everyday. Thus, art can intervene in my opinion on four levels:

- Exploration
- Monstration

- Therapy
- Upgrading.

Indeed, the study of Caribbean works shows that art can first act upstream on the functioning of our societies, through the exploration and understanding of what we are, who we are and why we are the way we are. The historical and historiographical approach, which is often the only one we have, does not provide Caribbean people with answers to many questions about their identity or identities, about ontological and social functions and dysfunctions, but also about values to which we could relate, especially from a spiritual point of view. This official history, which has been taught to us and which often remains the only source in many analyses, is, as we know, truncated and oriented, making no reference to the words of peoples who were deported, enslaved or exterminated. Thus, art in the Caribbean - and in this word art, I am including living arts denigrated by the West as primitive art, tradition or handicrafts - often serves as a basis of memory and history for Caribbean people. Songs, stories, paintings, ritual installations and carnival, for example, are filling the gap left by official history, they bring surfaces of expression to buried memories and allow people through intuitive or resurgence mechanisms to reconnect to the past and their Ancestors, to what is essential for the balance of each one and of course, for a good relationship with oneself and a positive reception of oneself and one's body.

Secondly, Art has a function of monstration and non-avoidance. The artist confronts us with our realities, our suffering, our dysfunctions and thus the work acquires a cathartic function. Devices of denial, devaluation and self-rejection implemented by the slave and colonial systems within plantations (and which are perpetuated in post-colonial societies or colonized, if we speak of a certain number of Caribbean islands, including Martinique and Guadeloupe), still have a very heavy impact on Caribbean populations, as we have seen, particularly in their relationship to their bodies. Indeed, the detestation of everything that does not correspond to an aesthetic ideal, of everything that would link us to non-European origins and particularly to Africa, has been taught to us in school, in the church, in institutions and through language: a European language, English, French, Spanish, full of colonial, racist terms and a Creole language with its own plantation vocabulary that is violent towards ourselves. All this, each of us have an intuitive perception of it, most of us know that violence is still being exerted on us and we very often feel frustration without being able to put words to it, without being able to dissect the meaning of what is happening inside us, without being able to name our emotions. The artist who is the sensitive skin of the people, as the philosopher René Ménil teaches us, can put words, senses and images on all our emotions and feelings. Performances, paintings, music, choreographies and plays bring out our buried emotions, they allow an exorcism of pain, they force us to face what we want to ignore and it is in this sense that the Caribbean work is cathartic.

Thirdly, Art has a therapeutic function, that is to say that through regular practice by a practitioner of an artistic discipline, the suffering person will be able to plug breaches opened by a sort of clumsiness, to exteriorize emotions that are not expressed, retained and contained. Derision and humour are often biases used in our societies allowing us to take distance and thus accept what hurts; however, it is sometimes necessary to approach the origin of suffering head-on, and in particular the non-acceptance of the body. Thus, dance and theatre in particular are art forms that allow the individual marked by the detestation of his skin colour, his shapes, his hair, and which are sometimes in the rejection of touch, in violence towards oneself (skin discolouration, hair loss) and even in self-destruction through the interference of addictive substances, to return to a healthy relationship with oneself.

And finally, fourthly, Art has a revalorizing function. Caribbean art has been about creating a new representation of the self, about constructing a new language that is not inferior, in short, about developing an aesthetics of value. Indeed, Aimé Césaire denounced in *Cahier d'un retour au pays natal* this imposture which consisted in making us believe that we were nothing in the world and that we had brought nothing to the world. The emergence of this Caribbean aesthetic which structures our music, our literature, our visual arts, which elaborates our masterpieces, our classicism, also elaborates us as human beings. The pride, the well-being, founding emotions and the sense of accomplishment that we feel in a concert, in front of a painting, a sculpture, an installation, watching a dancer restore the sacred, give us back the sense of ourselves, reveal us to ourselves, reconcile us with our bodies, teach us to look at ourselves with love, positively. Developing and appropriating this art that transcends us raises the individual and repairs people.

Conclusion

The Caribbean creator, I am speaking here of the artist who has taken a considerable step on himself and has gone down to the depths of his being to understand his relationship to the world and to the other, knows the **blés** and knows that he is carrying it with him. His creation is a reaction to **blés**, a therapy that applies to himself, but that is also meant for the other. The Caribbean artist has the will to understand these phenomena of internalization and somatization that lead to a sudden and violent rise of pain. He translates them as he feels them, and that is why his aesthetic is often an aesthetic of excess, as it is generated by the controlled irruption of evil and suffering. Popular wisdom perceives and names what in our urban centers we are no longer able to perceive or name; Art often knows how to take this perception on board. Caribbean art makes the Caribbean body speak; this body speaks of its suffering, this body speaks of its soul, this body speaks of its memory, this body speaks of its **blés**. And in doing so, it repairs itself.

REPARATIONS —An an urgent requirement for humanity

Duty of rememberance and denunciation of the chlordecone poisoning scandal in Martinique in the exhibition Tè Bwa, Glo by Patricia Donatien: an artistic plea for reparation and self-repair

By Rodolphe

Lecturer - Habilitated to supervise research

English Caribbean Studies, West Indies University

Report on the visit of the exhibition Tè Bwa, Glo[65] by Patricia Donatien, visible at the Galerie André Arsenec in Tropiques Atrium Scène nationale, from December 16 to January 4, 2020.

Tè Bwa, Glo appears as an exhibition created through keeping children of Martinique in mind, those of yesterday, today and tomorrow. Patricia Donatien denounces the genocidal poisoning of Martinique's water, the complicity and inertia in the face of this scandalous situation. But Tè Bwa, Glo goes further, to warn of the danger of disappearance that according to the artist is lurking for the people of Martinique.

Patricia Donatien's Tè Bwa, Glo welcomes the visitor with three canvases entitled respectively Tè, Bwa, and Glo which

---

[65] https://tropiques-atrium.fr/wp-content/uploads/2019/12/WEB-CATALOGUE-PD-DEC2019.pdf

introduce a multiform and poignant exhibition, created in an interrelation with the philosophy of the blè world of Martinique, and in an intertextuality with the song Té, bwa, glo by bèlè composer André Dru. André Dru's homage to nature metamorphoses into paintings ("La nati 1" and "La nati 2") in Patricia Donatien's creation.

But already the light of death coming from the triptych "Jénosid", attenuated by an impression of colorization, provokes fright, evoking the threat of an organized disappearance in full light by those who defile the mangrove-cradle of life.

Then, the Triptych "Yo kriminel" and the duet "Jistis", the series "Anba bwa," "Anba so," and "Fèy'o," contribute to the articulation of the discourse of Tè Bwa, Glo. Indeed, this triptych "Yo kriminel" as well as the duet "Jistis" are also created in an intertextuality with the bèlè song "Yo Kriminel" by Pierre Dru, who claims reparation for the victims of the poisoning of land and water by chlordecone.

In Tè Bwa, Glo paintings of various formats, altar, improbable sculpture are combined with a moving installation, "Take, all of you and drink from it", which denounces an institutionally authorized poisoning of water, carried out with great pomp and ceremony with the blessings of all those who knew. This gloomy picture of the situation in Martinique is however attenuated by a message of hope carried by the monumental work "The Colossus", made with photos of Schoelche's nature taken by Jacques Dijon, which is combined with another installation, entitled

"Little altar to ask forgiveness from the cut down tree", to invite people to reconnect with a nature that has the power to regenerate and to call on its fellow citizens to be actors of its regeneration.

If the general discourse of Tè Bwa, Glo articulates a denunciation of the international capitalism of monoculture sowing death, the canvas "Ago lé kiltivatè" pays homage to peasants who have a different relationship to tè, bwa, glo, than to that of "planters".

Those who are familiar with the artist's work will rediscover her approach and style, for an experience of beauty that is both refreshed and renewed. In fact, Patricia Donatien's canvases write the challenge of those who have left us without being respected. Those who have not been heard on the chlordecone invest Patricia Donatien's paintings. They impose themselves in this creation to challenge the community and demand justice. Their filigree appearance on canvases brings a certain renewal to Patricia Donatien's style.

The Poet was "the mouth of woes that have no mouth[66]," the hand of Patricia Donatien, who writes on the canvas those that were not heard on the chlordecone, who maybe

---

[66] Césaire, Aimé, *Cahier d'un retour au pays natal*. Paris : Présence africaine, 1956.

have joined the Un-honoured Ancestors, Ancestors without graves who died once in the very fields that have been now chlordeconated.

If for the Barbadian writer George Lamming, the Caribbean novelist is the historian of people's feelings, with the Triptych "Yo kriminel" and the duet "Jistis", by Tè Bwa Glo Patricia Donatien accesses the dimension of historian of a people's feelings made of blés to which new wounds are being inflicted.

In Tè Bwa, Glo, Patricia Donatien's commitment is served by an innovation in her practice that gives us a different and poignant experience of beauty in the series "Les gardiens de l'Alma", "Anba bwa," "Anba so", and "Fèy'o", paintings for which the artist uses a technique that combines acrylic painting on photographs of the undergrowth of Martinique, taken by musician-photographer Thierry Pivert and reprocessed using computer graphics.

Here, Patricia Donatien's innovative technique is at the service of the celebration of the woods and undergrowth of Martinique's land, which at the same time reveals the suffering beings that inhabit them.

Life and death, suffering and resources, Patricia Donatien projects us into the woods of the Country that conceal pain, threats and knowledge, memory and future, wandering and anger for "Anba bwa" and "Fèy'o", but also light, spirituality and hope for "Anba so".

After the experience of intimacy and matrilineal transmission proposed by the exhibition "Adie Julie et Moi", Tè Bwa, Glo projects us into the urgent concerns of the social, cultural and political world.

The title Tè Bwa, Glo, of this exhibition evokes the motto of the environmentalist association ASSAUPAMAR: "Tè, bwa, dlo". This intertextuality with Martinique's ecological discourse testifies to Patricia Donatien's commitment as an artist, but also to her involvement in the social field.

The reflection in which Tè Bwa, Glo plunges us, leads us to a dramatic observation. The words of the singer of negritude are tragically topical today in the midst of the International Decade for People of African Descent (2015-2024), the framework of action set up by the United Nations to invite its members to work in favour of people of African descent in three directions: Recognition, Justice and Development[67].

In the land of Aimé Césaire, which remains a land where racial segregation is supported and maintained by the French state, people of African descent are victims of

---

[67] O.N.U. A Decade devoted to people of African descent
https://www.un.org/fr/events/africandescentdecade/

U.N.O. Programme of mandated activities related to the International Decade of people of African descent
https://www.un.org/fr/events/africandescentdecade/plan-action.shtml

https://undocs.org/fr/A/RES/69/16

unrecognized racist crimes, are denied access to justice and are subject to economic injustice. (Complaints against those responsible for poisoning not investigated, prohibition of fishing without compensation, non-application of the polluter-pays principle in force in real France). Worse, those who are demanding recognition, justice and reparation are being repressed in a way that bears witness to the collusion between main beneficiaries of the crime of enslavement of Africans, the French State and Békés.

France's treatment of the Chloredecone poisoning of Martinicans and Guadeloupeans denounced by Tè Bwa, Glo is a clear indication of the exceptional violence in colonial lands, which is based on the conception that there is a superior white European humanity that has rights, and others whose humanity is being debated. It is this permanent exceptionality, which Aimé Césaire denounced in Discourse on Colonialism[68], that allowed the massive and genocidal deportation of Africans, for several centuries, including the so-called "Enlightenment". It is this same permanent exceptionality that has prevailed in decisions taken and renewed, in full knowledge of the danger of exposing Martinicans and Guadeloupeans to chlordecone. This permanent exceptional violence, from a human rights perspective, is practised by those who thought, and

---

[68] Césaire, Aimé. *Discours sur le colonialisme (Discourse on Colonialism) : followed by de Discours sur la négritude(Discourse on Blackness)*. Présence africaine, 1955

continue to think today, that there is not one humanity and that people of African descent do not belong to the same humanity as they do.

The occurrence of this chemical violence in the colonial racist exceptionalism (who cares they are just negroes) was possible because of the incomplete duty of memory and reparation of people of African descent, which did not allow them to escape the repetition of acts that are harmful to them. Indeed, since perpetrators and beneficiaries of the crimes of deportation and slavery did not acknowledge their acts, apologize or make reparation for the harm caused, guarantees of non-repetition[69] of acts harmful to their victims, specific to the reparation process[70], were not put in place.

---

[69] IX. Reparation for the harm inflicted

18. According to national and international law, for each case every victim of violation of human right and international human rights laws should be granted due compensation as said in the 19 to 23 principles under following forms : refund, compensation, rehabilitation, satisfaction and **guarantees of non-repetition**.

Fundamental Principles and instructions concerning the right to an judicial remedy and reparation Resolution adopted by the General Assembly on December 16th 2005 -60/147.

[70] See Resolution adopted by the General Assembly on December 16th 2005 - 60/147. *Fundamental Principles and instructions concerning the right to a judicial remedy and reparation to victims of blatant violation* of human rights and serious infringement of international human rights laws.

https://undocs.org/pdf?symbol=fr/A/RES/60/147

Tè Bwa, Glo rebels against the inertia of the vast majority of the population, dumbfounded by what is happening to them, but whose lack of reaction also testifies to the incompleteness of the duty of memory and reparation of people of African descent and to the lack of historical awareness produced by a Eurocentric institutional education and the promotion of a consumerist culture.

In the face of this inertia, the poignant interpellation of the triptych "Jénosid" constitutes a very strong statement on the seriousness of the situation in Martinique, whose population is, according to the artist, threatened with extinction. By choosing this name Patricia Donatien crosses swords with those who, in the face of this catastrophic situation, indulge themselves in technical and specious speeches and arguments seeking to understate the seriousness of things or to clear perpetrators or beneficiaries of poisoning: "correlation not scientifically established", "no direct link scientifically established", "authorizations obtained through legal lobbying" "we cannot speak of genocide, because according to the definition... acts must be committed with the intention of destroying, in whole or in part, a group... Genocide! states this triptych responding to those whom Aimé Césaire referred to as mumblers and obscurers.

"Just sweep away all obscurers, all inventors of subterfuge, all the mystifying charlatans, all gibberish-mongers. And do not try to find out whether these gentlemen are personally of good or bad faith ... the main thing being that their very random subjective good faith is in no way related to the objective and social scope of the bad work they do as watchdogs of colonialism71.

Beyond the emotion, "Jenosid" invites us to reflect on the concerted character of the poisoning. How could several decades of concerted action, strategies, and the search for derogatory means to use this molecule whose dangerousness was known not be considered as unintentional? It is indeed an "intentional submission" of the people of Martinique and Guadeloupe "to conditions of existence that should lead to their total or partial physical destruction". It is indeed "serious bodily or mental harm to members of the group", two crimes included in the definition of genocide established by the UN in the 1948 Convention. The people of Martinique were victims of two of the crimes included in this definition of genocide, but these crimes should not qualify as genocide because they were not committed with the intent to destroy them.

"Jenosid" urges us to sweep away these nuances so regularly mobilized by obscurers, inventors of subterfuge, mystifying charlatans, gibberish handlers who, always in a "very random subjective good faith", set about the evil task of euphemising racist colonial crimes.

---

[71] Césaire, Aimé. *Discours sur le colonialisme,* 38-39

Their objections are, moreover, easily invalidated, because the definition of the notion of genocide is neither fixed nor definitive, it is even under debate. Indeed, if one sticks to the 20th century's conception of genocide, which recognizes only four genocides, "it becomes clear that the word 'genocide' is an enumeration72 and has no definition73. (The genocide of Armenians by the Young Turkish Government, the genocide of Jews by Nazi Germany, the genocide in Cambodia by the Khmer Rouge and the genocide of the Rwandan Tutsi by the Rwandan Hutu74).

Moreover, "since we are not sticking to the 20th century, we are forced to give a second definition to genocide [...] which insists on effective extermination75", says Ninon Grangé. Grangé states that "the essence of genocide, as a historical

---

[72] Convention for the Prevention and the Punishment of the crime of Genocide 1948 UN General Assembly.

In the present Convention Genocide is listed in the following acts, committed with the intent to destroy in the whole or in part a national; ethnic, racial or religious group such as :
a) Murdering group members ;
b) Serious bodily or mental harm to members of the group ;
c) Deliberately inflicting on a group conditions of life calculated to bring about its physical destruction in whole or in part ;
d) Measures intended to prevent births to members of a group ;
e) Forcibly transferring children of a group to another group.
[73] **Ninon** GRANGÉ, « Les génocides et l'état de guerre » « Genocides and the state of war », *Astérion* [En ligne], 6 | 2009, mis en ligne le 03 avril 2009, consulted on December 30, 2019. URL :
[74] **Ninon** GRANGÉ, « Les génocides et l'état de guerre », *Astérion*
[75] **Ninon** GRANGÉ, « Les génocides et l'état de guerre », *Astérion* :

event, is extermination. She adds that a distinction is sometimes made between extermination intent and strategic extermination. This strategic extermination is often present in cases of colonial genocides76.

Thus, today, in order to assess the genocidal nature of an extermination, "the distinction by intention does not appear to be decisive". Indeed, particularly in the context of colonization, the extermination of a group may be a secondary objective in the conquest of a territory77.

If we examine a few situations not recognized as genocides to date through the 1948 Convention on the Prevention and Punishment of the Crime of Genocide, without resorting to the now invalidated criterion of the "primary intention to exterminate a group or a people", the trafficking in Africans does indeed constitute genocide, since it produces the result, "the partial physical destruction" of the Peoples of

---

[76] About colonial genocide : « [...] in the XIXth century, populations captured are considered as not organized politically, as they usually live far from everything so, they might be conquerred – there lies the difference between conquerring and colonizing – so that the State feels itself at home and therefore a priori authorizes itself to settle in places considered as vacant. Because of that, lands thus subjected to be colonized, are occupied in imagination prior to be effectively conquerred, occupied, administered. **Ninon** GRANGÉ, "Genocides and the state of war", *Astérion*

[77] The political intent to exterminate a group is non existing, not programmed and constitutive of political boundaries, it can be an extreme winning strategy of a territory or at best secondary to the goals. **Ninon** GRANGÉ, « Genocides and the state of war », *Astérion*.

West Africa78 as well as "serious bodily or mental harm" to their members.

Similarly, the living conditions on the slave plantations in the Caribbean do indeed constitute those of a genocide of Africans, since they consist of the "intentional submission of the group to conditions of existence that are likely to bring about its total or partial physical destruction" (extraordinary mortality caused by working from sunrise to sunset). This intentional submission is linked to the "serious physical or mental harm to the members of the group" constituted by the torture of the African upon his arrival in the Caribbean, known as "creolization". Thus, making the African fit to work on the plantation consisted of committing a number of crimes included in the list of crimes of genocide. Creolization meant making an African into a slave, after treatment that consisted of "destroying, in whole or in part, a national, ethnic, racial or religious group".

For a postcolonial redefinition of genocide

This reflection to which this triptych "Jenosid" obliges us offers us the opportunity for a postcolonial redefinition of genocide. We thus propose that we consider as genocide, crimes defined by the UN convention of 1948, which are the product of a convergence of means and practices put in place by a State, a dominant group or groups or under their

---

[78] Around 12 million deportees

responsibility, and which produce a genocidal result of extermination.

Considering that Martinique loses annually (through organized action) several thousands of young people, that the fertility of the people of Martinique is impacted by chlordecone poisoning, that many people die from various cancers that are increasing exponentially, that the water and the land have been poisoned, and that a State ethnic immigration is organized towards this country (see the genocide by substitution of Kanaky), how can the situation in Martinique not be read as that of genocide, that is to say, the product of a convergence of means and practices put in place by a dominant group or groups under their control or responsibility which intentionally subject the people of Martinique to conditions of existence that are intended to bring about their total or partial physical destruction, and are causing "serious harm to their physical or mental integrity?

Tè Bwa, Glo thus intervenes in the social debate of the moment, as a duty to remember, in the continuation of the reflection on memory to which the 201379 Soul Amere exhibition already invited us. Patricia Donatien is a committed artist and critic, an art theorist and a university professor. Today, she places the knowledge of scholars and people, built and refined over several decades (since

---

[79] Donatien Patricia, *Soul Amère :* painting exhibition & installations, Galerie Arsenec Atrium, Fort de France, February 2013.

Africobra80), at the service of the people, of her people, whom she summons to react.

---

[80] Donatien-Yssa, Patricia. *Africobra : aesthetics and an expression of an ideology of African Americans plastic expression : wall of respect*. Diss. Université de Lille III, ANRT, 1995.

See also : Donatien-Yssa, Patricia. *The blés exorcism* . Éditions Le Manuscrit, 2007.

Three examples of victims of racial discrimination fighting for respect for their humanity and their people: "justice and reparation".

What reparations for "Renault's discriminated employees" following the decision of the UN Committee on the Elimination of Racial Discrimination?

By Joby Valente

(source Laurent Gabaroum)

President of the Movement for a New Humanity

Vice President of the Collectif des Filles et Fils d'Africains Déportés (Collective of Daughters and sons of African Deportees)

The UN International Convention on the Elimination of All Forms of Racial Discrimination (CERD) obliges States Parties to eliminate all forms of racial discrimination and promote understanding between races. It defines racial discrimination as "*any distinction, exclusion, restriction or preference based on race, colour, descent, or national or ethnic origin which has the purpose or effect of nullifying or impairing the recognition, enjoyment or exercise, on an equal footing, of human rights and fundamental freedoms in the political, economic, social, cultural or any other field of public life*".

Since 2000, Renault employees have brought cases before the UN Committee on the Elimination of Racial Discrimination, claiming to be victims of violations of their rights under the Convention, particularly with regard to compensation.

Requests of Mr. Lucien Stanislas BRELEUR and Mr. Daniel KOTOR.

Mr. Lucien Stanislas BRELEUR is a French citizen of Martinique origin.

When he joined the company in 1971, he worked as an automotive electrician.

When he retired on December 1, 2003, he was then qualified as a technical service employee, senior category.

As for Mr. Daniel KOTOR, he is French of Togolese origin.

Hired in 1971 as an automobile mechanic and when retired in February 2004, he was a qualified store manager, with the status of supervisor.

All along their activity, the latters have suffered significant discrimination in the development of their respective professional careers.

It is in this context that, by decision of 20 March 2003, they referred the matter to the Boulogne-Billancourt industrial tribunal (Conseil de prud'hommes) in order to get themselves repositioned in coefficients that should have been theirs and obtain the payment of damages.

In a partially overturning judgment of April 2, 2008, the Versailles Court of Appeal upheld their claims on the grounds that Renault had failed to prove that the difference in treatment between BRELEUR and KOTOR and employees in a comparable situation was *"justified by objective factors unrelated to any discrimination based on actual or supposed membership or non-membership of an ethnic group, nation or race"*.

Consequently, in partially reversing the judgment dated December 12, 2005 and ruling again, the Versailles Court of Appeals has ordered Société Renault to proceed payment of :

- 80,000 in compensation for his prejudice to his career and material damages to Mr. BRELEUR and 8,000 as a compensation for his moral suffering.

- 60,000 in compensation for his prejudice to his career and material damages to Mr. KOTOR and 8,000 as a compensation for his moral suffering.

The Court of Appeal confirmed, for the rest, provisions of the judgment undertaken and, in addition :

- ordered the repositioning of Mr. BRELEUR at coefficient 260 from 1985 to 1989, then 285 from 1990 to 1999, then at coefficient 305 from 2000 until his retirement in December 2003.

- ordered the repositioning of Mr. KOTOR at a factor of 260 from 1985 to 1989, then 285 from 1990 to 1999, then 305 from 2000 until his retirement in February 2004.

In other words, the Versailles Court of Appeal had intended to grant them a cumulative repositioning in the situation that should have been theirs, as well as damages and interest.

Had it been otherwise, it would have been difficult to understand why the Court of Appeal of Versailles did not simply award Mr. BRELEUR and Mr. KOTOR damages.

However, it must be acknowledged that in this case, the Court was careful to add that Mr. BRELEUR and Mr. KOTOR had to be repositioned, which was part of the strictest respect for the principle of full reparation.

Renault believed that it could comply with the judgment only in part, by merely paying Mr. BRELEUR and Mr KOTOR sums allocated to them respectively by the Court of Appeal, without repositioning them in accordance with coefficients adopted in the judgment.

It is under these conditions that, by deed dated November 28, 2008, Mr. BRELEUR and Mr. KOTOR were obliged to refer the matter to the enforcement judge in Nanterre, in order for him to order Renault to issue them with an employment certificate in accordance with the repositioning pronounced by the Versailles Court of Appeal.

By judgment dated March 17, 2009, the enforcement judge declared himself to have no jurisdiction.

By judgment dated May 6, 2010, the Versailles Court of Appeal confirmed the judgment in all its provisions.

In view of the real prejudice suffered by Mr. BRELEUR and Mr. KOTOR in the calculation of their pension rights, due to Renault's failure to fulfil its obligation to reposition, the latter brought the matter before the Versailles enforcement judge by order dated June 22, 2011 for the purpose of ordering that the obligation to reposition them be accompanied by a penalty payment of 1,000 euros per day of delay.

By judgment of 25 October 2011, the enforcement judge of the Versailles Regional Court declared itself incompetent in favour of the enforcement judge of Nanterre.

In a judgment rendered on July 3, 2012, the Nanterre enforcement judge dismissed Mr. BRELEUR and Mr. KOTOR's claims, on the grounds that they would have been res judicata under the judgment rendered on April 2, 2008 by the Versailles Court of Appeals.

Mr. BRELEUR and Mr. KOTOR appealed against this decision.

By judgment dated September 5, 2013, the Versailles Court of Appeals confirmed in full the judgment undertaken and declared inadmissible the request that a penalty payment be added to the obligation to reposition.

The Court of Appeal also referred Mr. BRELEUR and Mr. KOTOR to appeal before any court having jurisdiction on the merits, on the grounds that "*the authority of res judicata could not be opposed to a request for production of documents by the interested parties*".

Mr. BRELEUR and Mr. KOTOR appealed in cassation.

On December 4, 2014, the 2nd civil division of the Court of Cassation overturned this decision, in accordance with Articles L213-6 and L131-1 of the Code of Civil Enforcement Procedures.

Ruling after referral to the Supreme Court, the Versailles Court of Appeal, in a decision dated September 24, 2015, overturned the enforcement judge's decision of July 3, 2012.

Ruling again, it first declared admissible the request presented by Mr. BRELEUR and Mr. KOTOR for a penalty payment to be added to the obligation to reposition ordered by the previous decision of the Court of Appeal of VERSAILLES dated April 2, 2008.

However, it dismissed their claim on the merits on the grounds, among others, that the Court of Appeal would have compensated the employee's entire loss by awarding damages alone, which would include the consequences of the repositioning of Mr. BRELEUR and Mr. KOTOR.

Mr. BRELEUR and Mr. KOTOR appealed against this decision to the Supreme Court of Appeal.

In a decision dated December 1, 2016, the 2nd Civil Chamber of the Court of Cassation rejected the appeal on the basis of the provisions of Article 1014 of the Code of Civil Procedure, which authorizes it to rule without giving reasons when it considers that the ground or grounds of cassation invoked in support of the appeal are clearly not such as to lead to cassation.

France, having ratified the International Convention on the Elimination of All Forms of Racial Discrimination, is bound to respect it and to ensure that it is respected.

For the record, the discrimination suffered by Mr. BRELEUR and Mr. KOTOR on the grounds of their membership to an ethnic group, nation or race was recognized by a final judgment having the force of res judicata, handed down on 2 April 2008 by the Court of Appeal of Versailles.

It will be recalled that in 1945, Renault underwent a "sanctioned nationalization" for collaboration with Nazi Germany, which became the Régie Nationale des Usines Renault. Having become a Société Anonyme in 1990, the French State held 80% of the capital until 1996. Today, it is the reference shareholder.

The French State must therefore be held accountable for the racial discrimination suffered by Mr. BRELEUR and Mr. KOTOR since it has failed to ensure that Renault complies with the International Convention on the Elimination of All Forms of Racial Discrimination, which it signed and ratified even though it is well known that discriminatory practices abound against employees of non-European descent.

Internal documents have been made public which attest to the systematization of these discriminatory practices, including the so-called "ESCADRE" system, which implements an "ethnic codification" of employees structured around skin colour and ethnic origins.

An internal note states that "**Blacks are a source of tension in the company**", that "**Blacks are the most difficult workers to assimilate into the French company (...)**" or that " **the worst performers in terms of the quality module of adaptation to work in the company are undoubtedly black Africans and Algerians, Moroccans and Tunisians, closely followed by workers from the overseas districts**".

The French State's tolerance of such discriminatory practices has been highly damaging, since Mr. BRELEUR and Mr. KOTOR have been called "**monkey**" and "**nigger bugger**" by their superiors.

In 2017, after exhausting domestic remedies, Mr. Stanislas Lucien BRELEUR and Mr. Daniel KOTOR referred the matter to the UN Committee on the Elimination of Racial Discrimination.

The request of Mr. Laurent GABAROUM

Laurent GABAROUM, a Frenchman of Chadian origin, joined the Régie Nationale des Usines Renault on 15th July 1975, under a permanent contract, as a Renault Production Agent, category B.

At the same time, he was pursuing graduate studies in law and economics, which were to lead him to a doctorate in law.

Discriminatory practices against Laurent GABAROUM began in the 1980s when he revealed to the Régie Nationale des Usines Renault that he was preparing a Post-Graduate Degree in Management, Transport and Business Logistics and a Doctoral thesis in law.

In 1985, after some painful events, Mr. Laurent GABAROUM was promoted to executive level.

However, the Renault company, hostile to the presence of Blacks within the company's management, openly and publicly challenged Mr. Laurent GABAROUM on the legitimacy of his French nationality on the grounds that "*The hen has never laid black eggs*" and organized his forced return to Africa for a reconversion to farming in order to help feed his "black brothers who are starving".

On 19 March 2003, Mr. Laurent GABAROUM referred the matter to the Paris Prud'hommes Council for recognition of the existence of racial discrimination, of which he considers to be the object.

On January 11, 2005, the Paris Employment Tribunal, sitting in a tie-breaking vote, ordered Renault to pay Mr.

Laurent GABAROUM the sum of €120,000 for *"failure to perform his employment contract in good faith"*. However, it failed to take into account the racial dimension of the discrimination which motivated this "failure to perform loyally".

Mr. Laurent GABAROUM appealed against the said judgment and requested a complete reversal of the decision.

In its decision of September 12, 2006, the Paris Court of Appeal reversed the judgment and ordered Mr. Laurent GABAROUM to reimburse Renault for 120,000 euros.

In view of the elliptical reasoning of the September 12, 2006 ruling, Mr. Laurent Gabaroum appealed to the Supreme Court of Appeal.

It will be recalled that in order to abuse the good faith of the judges and successfully deny the absence of any racial discrimination against Mr. Laurent GABAROUM, Renault *company blackened, by photocopying, the photos of white executives that it presented to the Paris Court of Appeal as black executives*.

By an unjustified decision of September 22, 2011, the Court of Cassation dismissed the appeal without explaining the objective reasons for which it would not have been admitted.

On 19 March 2012, Mr. Laurent GABAROUM filed an application before the UN Committee on the Elimination of Racial Discrimination.

On 10 May 2016, in its decision under article 14 of the Convention, the UN Committee on the Elimination of Racial Discrimination concluded that *"facts before revealing a violation by the State party of articles 2 and 6 of the Convention"*.

In a letter dated 18 August 2016, Mr. Laurent GABAROUM expressed to the UN Committee on the Elimination of Racial Discrimination the fundamental principle concerning the right to reparation of flagrant victims of international human rights law in matters of racial discrimination.

In a letter dated September 12, 2016, Mr. Laurent GABAROUM communicated the decision of the UN Committee on the Elimination of Racial Discrimination to the Versailles Court of Appeal and to Renault, informing them that *"In application of the provisions of resolution 60/147 of December 16, 2005 of the UN General Assembly, the decision of the UN Human Rights Committee confers on Mr. GABAROUM a right to compensation for the prejudice resulting from the violation of Articles 2 and 6 of the UN Convention, which makes the continuation of the appeal procedure pointless"*.

Renault's desire to free itself from the obligation to make full reparation for damage

Article L.1132-4 of the Labour Code establishes a principle of nullity of all discriminatory measures, which implies, therefore, that the employee who is the victim of discrimination should be granted the advantage or situation that should have been due to him or her.

The case law thus logically considers that compensation for discrimination *"requires that the person who suffered it be placed in a situation where he would have been had the harmful conduct not occurred"* (Soc. 23 November 2005, Bull. V, no. 332; see also for a hypothesis where the employee was entitled to be reclassified in the remuneration coefficient that he would have reached in the absence of discrimination, Soc. 28 September 2011, no. 10-14.662).

In this respect**, the High Court recalls with constancy that the repositioning of employees is an integral part of full reparation** (Soc. 23 November 2005, Bull. No. 332), *"that after having acknowledged the existence of discrimination in the employee's career development"*, the judges on the merits must, *"by referring to the classification of jobs provided for in the undertaking decide on a reclassification of the person concerned"* (Soc. 24 February 2004, No. 01-46.499).

The need to fully compensate the damages suffered by the employee cannot thus be reduced to the payment of damages alone, but must lead to the reclassification of the employee who is the victim of discrimination, without his retirement being an obstacle to his repositioning (Soc. 30 June 2011, n° 09-71.538).

It is therefore up to the trial judges to determine what classification the employee would have reached if he or she had had a normal career and to order, as compensation, that he or she be reassigned to that classification (Soc. 14 March 2012, No. 11-11.308; Soc. 20 March 2013, No. 11-27.432).

And there is no doubt that the employee's repositioning, in addition to the payment of damages, necessarily implies that he or she be issued with work certificates and pay slips corrected in accordance with the situation in which he or she was repositioned as full compensation for the discrimination suffered.

These principles have, however, been completely lost sight of to the detriment of Mr. BRELEUR and Mr. KOTOR.

In the same vein, Renault has multiplied specious interpretations of the decision of the UN Committee on the Elimination of Racial Discrimination, thus excluding any application of the provisions of resolution 60/147 of December 16, 2005 of the UN General Assembly conferring on Mr. Laurent GABAROUM a right to compensation for the prejudice resulting from the violation of articles 2 and 6 of the UN Convention.

Faced with this unprecedented situation, initiatives are currently underway to enable victims of Renault's discriminatory practices to have their rights to reparation honoured.

Afterword: MIR's appeal to all descendants of deported Africans and to all Africans on the continent

The analysis of the texts published in this book shows that Reparation must first of all be inscribed in a vision of liberation of Thought and of the Man, which implies a vast enterprise of restructuring the dehumanized and enslaved Human being, in his spiritual dimension and in his dignity as a human being.

It must be a tool at the service of the total liberation and fulfilment of dominated peoples, predated by the West, which has arrogated to itself the right to deny them their humanity.

For our people, reparation is therefore fundamental to regaining true freedom, that is to say, freedom of the mind, the freedom to be able to express a thought that is as free as possible, the fruit of inner deliberation free from alienation.

Time has come to put an end to this denial of reality on the part of our peoples, who for too long have refused to see the grave consequences of crimes that have lasted for centuries.

The Europeans who today are trying to minimise them can no longer erase the stench of guilt and responsibility that led them to officially acknowledge these crimes, while continuing to adopt aggressive attitudes towards the black people who are the victims.

The descendants of deported Africans and the Africans of the continent, who for too long have been sparing Europe because of their situation of economic dependence, cannot, however, forget that it is this same Europe that is at the root of the dramatic situation they are experiencing.

The time has come for us to speak with ONE VOICE AND DEMAND IN THE NAME OF HUMANITY, that the West should repair the crimes against humanity committed against our peoples.

The restoration of a Humanity reconciled with itself requires total, integral and global reparation.

For this reason, we call ON ALL AFRICANS FROM AFRICA AND THE DIASPORA TO JOIN THE ACTION IN REPAIR OF THE MIR, both in a personal capacity and as rightful beneficiaries of the victims of both crimes in new procedures that we are going to put in place in order to achieve the establishment of this necessary reparation, a guarantee of reconciliation and the fulfilment of all people.

The International Reparation Movement

Introducing MIR International Movement for Reparations

Created by people of African descent from the Continent and the Diaspora, the International Movement for Reparations has notably initiated since 2001 the "*Convoys for Reparations*" *(Konvwa pou reparasyon)* in Martinique, Guadeloupe and French Guiana in collaboration with speakers from neighbouring countries (ICNP of Guadeloupe...) and supported the Reparation Movement of Reunion carried by deported children.

MIR members have participated in numerous international conferences in the Americas and on the African continent with a view to advancing the issue of Reparations in various international forums (UN, UNESCO, CARICOM, AU...).

Since 2018, the MIR has initiated Konvwa pou reparasyon in Africa. The first one has taken place in April 2018 in Senegal and the second one in Benin in August 2019. The role of these konvwa is to reconcile the children of the diaspora with the Kama land and to bring the issue of reparations to the debate of Africans on the continent. This reconnection led to the creation of the MIR Senegal in May 2019.

The International Movement for Reparations (MIR) is an anti-imperialist, environmentalist and anti-discrimination movement. It adheres to the principle adopted at the World Conference Against Racism in Durban (2001), i.e., in all struggles, priority should be given to the "voice of the victims". The MIR echoes the adoption of the Taubira law (2001) and is the first organization to have filed a complaint against the French State calling for reparations for slavery, in May 2005. The MIR promotes the concept of **three "R"** (**Recognition, Reparation and Reconciliation**), which are defined as follows:

Recognition: The Western world must recognize the historical debt it owes to the people of Africa and, in general, to all people who were enslaved. The French Republic has already taken a first step (Taubira law). But much remains to be done...

Reparation: This debt must be paid, in one way or another, through reconstruction work and by compensating the victims and the daughters and sons of the victims.

Reconciliation: Together moving forward in the same direction, without forgetting the past.

MIR Books

23 MAY 2005
First assignment of a colonial State in Reparation
Edition of the MIR

10 MAY 2011
French National Commemoration MEMORANDUM OF THE NEGERIAN TREATY OF SLAVERY AND THE ABOLITION OF THEIR ABOLITIONS
MIR Publication